DRIED FLOWERS FOR ALL SEASONS

DRIED FLOWERS FOR ALL SEASONS

Betty Smith Wiita

PHOTOGRAPHS BY
Kristina Gustafson Hofmann

ILLUSTRATIONS BY
Elsie Burkhardt Tamson

 **VAN NOSTRAND REINHOLD COMPANY**
New York Cincinnati Toronto London Melbourne

DEDICATION

Library of Congress Catalog Card
Number 82-2801
ISBN 0-442-24559-9

Printed in the United States

Published by
Van Nostrand Reinhold Company Inc.
135 West 50th Street
New York, NY 10020

Van Nostrand Reinhold
Company Limited
Molly Millars Lane
Wokingham, Berkshire
England RG11 2PY

Van Nostrand Reinhold
Australia Pty. Ltd.
480 Latrobe Street
Melbourne, Victoria 3000
Australia

Macmillan of Canada
Division of Gage Publishing Limited
164 Commander Boulevard
Agincourt, Ontario M1S 3C7, Canada

16 15 14 13 12 11 10 9 8 7 6 5 4 3 2

Library of Congress Cataloging in Publication Data

Wiita, Betty Smith.
 Dried flowers for all seasons.

 Includes index.
 1. Dried flower arrangement. 2. Flowers—Drying.
I. Title.
SB449.3.D7W54   745.92   82-2801
ISBN 0-442-24559-9   AACR2

To Emma Stark Smith, *ma merveilleux petite mère*, whose research, assistance, and encouragement made this book possible.

To my father, George A. Smith, for his confidence and support.

And, in loving memory of Aliki A. Glumidge, a beautiful friend who would have loved this book.

CONTENTS

ACKNOWLEDGMENTS

Without the gentle encouragement of such friends as Joanne Greene Shivers; June H. Rotker; Julia and Wendell Leigh; Harry and Vivi Gustafson; Ceil Kozek, *Gloucester County Times;* Carmen Maria and Esteban Fuertes; Joyce Bennett, Editor of *Crafts* magazine; Nancy Tosh, Editor of *Crafts 'n Things* magazine; Ann Dirrigl, Jane Ross, and Pat Van Note of *Better Homes and Gardens;* Bob Grant of WMCA-N.Y.; Gary Geers of KYW-TV; W. Carter Merbreier (Captain Noah) of WPVI-TV; Marion Savoca of Rutgers' Horticultural and Forestry Department; Virginia Reynolds and Al Dolinski for sharing their wonderful flower farms with me; Linda and Rev. Stanley Phillips; without the expertise of my brother, Gerald A. Smith, with the tape recordings and equipment, and without the assistance with the research by Malcom R. "Bud" Harrison, Rutgers' Extension Specialist in Floriculture; Ray Battle and Bob Langlois, County Agents for Rutgers' Extension Service in Agriculture; Dr. George L. Wulster, Department of Floriculture at Rutgers University; Lois Stringer and Linda D. Harris, Assistant Horticulturist, of the W. Atlee Burpee Company; Albert D. Addis, Director of McCowan Memorial Library; the staff of Longwood Gardens who are never too busy to share their horticultural wisdom; the library staff of the Morris Arboretum of the University of Pennsylvania; Barbara C. Dean, Assistant Librarian of the Colonial Williamsburg Foundation; the Society of American Florists; Brooklyn Botanic Gardens library; the libraries of the Pennsylvania Horticultural Society and American Swedish Historical Museum in Philadelphia, this book might still be only a dream.

AND . . . *very special* bouquets to Susan Gies, Senior Editor, Van Nostrand Reinhold, for her patience and guidance in the preparation and production of this text; Jean Lynch for her enthusiastic typing of the manuscript; my wonderful children who will finally see the book as a reality instead of a mere figment of their mother's imagination; my dear friends Kris Hofmann for her many hours of painstaking photography and Elsie Tamson for her magnificent sketches and illustrations and, finally, Milan Glumidge for his understanding, hospitality, and many kindnesses to Kris and me at beautiful Bluebeard's Castle during the final days.

My deepest and eternal gratitude to you all.

INTRODUCTION

Have you ever felt a bit saddened at seeing a lovely arrangement of fresh flowers wilt and fade away? Have you ever wished you could keep a velvet-petaled rose fresh and beautiful forever? Well, forever is a very long time, but there are ways of preserving nature's treasures for many years of enjoyment, and that's what this book is all about.

Traditionally, dried arrangements are associated with the harvest time of the year. In *Dried Flowers for All Seasons*, you will explore the many varieties and colors of plant material that dry well for arrangements to be enjoyed all year round. Many of the natural materials covered in this book are wildlings, Mother Nature's gifts to you. Other flowers and materials suitable for drying and preservation can be grown in your garden, even if your garden consists of just a few flower boxes on the porch or patio.

Nothing made by man can possibly approach the infinite varieties, colors, and unusual textures produced in nature. As you begin working in this fascinating medium, you will become aware of nature's exceptional beauty. There will be disappointments along the way, as you discover the individual characteristics related to drying hundreds of varieties of flowers, leaves, ferns, pods, cones, and fruits, but remember what someone once said: "If you have tried to do something and failed, you are vastly better off than if you had tried to do nothing and succeeded." Your successes will far outnumber your disappointments with just a little practice, some experimentation, and frequent reference to this book.

In this book, I have introduced new methods of drying flowers and leaves that are absolutely terrific! Included are a total of six different techniques of preserving flowers, including two original methods of using the microwave oven to dry them, plus techniques for air drying, pressing, and capturing the scents of flowers.

The book is arranged in a logical sequence to ease beginners into this fascinating art and to aid well-seasoned enthusiasts in reviewing some ideas they may have forgotten and then rapidly updating them in the newest techniques.

The separation of projects by season provides you with an orderly "game plan." The projects are not the usual flowers-in-a-vase type. A quick thumbing through of the book will tell you that, yet they are all easy to construct. These bouquets, arrangements, and wreaths are practical for use as gifts and make excellent holiday and home decor accent pieces.

I first became interested in trying to preserve flowers while working as private secretary for the famous Danish pianist-humorist, Victor Borge. I had been living in the Caribbean for years, perennially surrounded by exotic blooms of every description. Upon arriving at Vibo Farms, the Borge estate in Southbury, Connecticut, I found snow so deep that it had drifted up to the eaves of the house. Of course, there was not a flower to be seen out of doors, but inside the Borges' lovely home, Mrs. Borge, Sanna, made sure there were always fresh bouquets of flowers in evidence, as well as dried arrangements, which blended well with their Early American decor.

As spring arrived, Vibo Farms ("Vi" for Victor and "bo" for Borge) looked as though it had been transplanted to Holland, a result of Sanna Borge's expert supervision of the gardening staff at bulb-planting time. Tulips of every color and variety edged the lake, pond, walkways, and riding ring. Daffodils, narcissus, jonquils, and grape hyacinths were everywhere! Suddenly, I was determined to try to preserve this fleeting beauty.

My first attempt at drying a daffodil was less than successful. I had used a combination of Borax, white cornmeal, and salt, and must have overlooked some moisture on the flower petals. The compound cemented itself to the daffodil and the flower crumbled as I tried to dust it off. However, the color of the bloom was excellent, so I was encouraged to try again. My second experiment into this intriguing art brought the satisfaction I was looking for. I used silica gel, made certain the flowers were completely dry to the touch, experimented a little with the timing, and was able to dry enough daffodils to create a bouquet arrangement that lasted many months longer than their outdoor blooming cousins.

As spring rushed on, the next flowers I tried drying were the lilacs. I found they would dry well simply by hanging them to air dry. They shriveled as they dried, but held a very good, strong color *if* they had been hung to dry when they were dry to the touch. If there was the least amount of dew on the florets, they would dry with a reddish-brown water stain which detracted considerably from the flower. (Air-dried lilacs can add an excellent "pick up" color and shape to spring and colonial arrangements.)

I also experimented with drying lilacs in silica gel. Although the flower heads flattened in my first attempts, I soon learned to prop up the heads with a small piece of cardboard bent into a tent shape. This allowed the silica gel to "slide" under the flower head, slowly building up around it, supporting it, and then finally covering it. With this cardboard support, the lilacs were no longer crushed by the weight of the gel, and the results were exhilarating. I now had lilacs to add to my daffodil display.

My third attempt at preserving the floral fantasyland at Vibo Farms was to try drying a peony. In the center of the five-hundred-acre estate, there is a two-acre lake encircled with the most beautiful, perfectly shaped peonies I have ever seen. They grew close to the edge of the lake, reflecting in the water and creating a breathtaking view. Because peonies are so large and their petals quite compacted, I was not really confident of my success. I made sure the peony to be dried was picked on a very dry day and was a newly opened blossom (for strong petal structure and vibrant color), and I made sure my silica gel was freshly oven-dried. After carefully burying the peony in the silica gel and leaving it undisturbed for a week, I was amazed to find I had dried a flower every bit as fresh looking as the ones surrounding the lake. The only thing missing was the heavenly scent that permeated the entire outdoors.

From that moment on, there was no stopping me. My enthusiasm for experimenting with and reading about possible ways of preserving the beauty of the natural world—pine cones, woody pods, flowers, berries, leaves, moss, fern, and lichen—was endless. I hope you too will catch some of this enthusiasm and will begin, with this book, to see the great outdoors in a way you never did before. Delving into the mysteries of plant preservation can be a new and gratifying experience, a never-ending adventure.

TECHNIQUES

There are many methods of drying and preserving flowers and foliage. Some people still use the Borax, cornmeal, and salt method. Others swear by sand. Still others prefer cat litter, perlite, antifreeze, and oolitic sand.

The six methods of flower preservation described in this chapter are those I have found to be the most dependable in producing the best quality preserved material, time after time.

Because we live in such an "instant society," I have experimented with speeding up the drying processes and have come up with new methods. These are described under Preheated Silica Gel, Silica Gel and the Microwave Oven, and The Microwave Oven Alone. Of course, if you do not have a microwave oven, you may dry out and preheat silica gel in a conventional oven (at 250°F.). In the Pressing Flowers section you will find two methods of speeding up the preservation of flowers by pressing. Instead of taking two to three weeks to press your flowers, you can press them in a matter of minutes and be ready to work with them in a project in no time!

Not all plant material responds well to every method. The Quick Reference Chart at the back of the book will tell you which methods are best for the particular plant material you wish to preserve.

ORGANIZATION OF TOOLS AND SUPPLIES

It saves time and makes working with dried materials more fun if all your tools, supplies, and containers are kept in one handy location. Perhaps you have a shelf or two in a utility closet that you can devote to this worthwhile cause. You will save yourself endless hours of searching for the proper tools or materials, if you establish your supply area now. Once you have found this treasured space and assigned it to your new hobby, gather the following items.

Containers

A good assortment of containers is essential and something to be accumulated over a period of time. You will want to include baskets of all sizes, some containers of brass, pewter, wood, china, porcelain, ceramic, glass, crystal, or silver. You may find some of these items in your china cabinet, attic, basement, or perhaps at a flea market. Whatever the type of container, always be certain when using it that it complements the arrangement rather than detracts from it. Glance through the pages of this book to get an idea of some of the containers I've used.

Floral Foam

This material usually comes in a brick shape, but it can be cut into any size needed. The foam is fastened inside the container and flower stems are inserted into it, to make positioning of the flowers easier. You may have seen the green foam, called Oasis, in fresh flower arrangements. The same company manufactures a brown foam called Sahara for use with dried flowers. I find that both the green and brown foam work equally well. Ultra-Foam is another floral foam product that works especially well with heavy stems, such as tree branches, and with thick-stemmed flowers, the type you might use in a large arrangement. These three foams have the proper density to work well with the dehydrated, brittle stems of dried flowers. Floral foam is available at hobby and floral-supply stores. (See Sources.)

Wreath Rings, Flat wire Rings, and Box Rings

These are made of floral foam, styrofoam, or wire. There are two types of wire rings; one is called a flat wire ring and the other a box ring. All are available in craft and floral-supply stores. (See Sources.)

Floral Wires

These are sold by weight and number in hobby and floral-supply stores. The thickest wire has the lowest number. I keep #18 on hand for heavy stems, #20 and #22 for medium and lightweight stems, and #26 for corsage work.

Adhesives

You will want to keep a can of rubber cement available for anchoring floral foam to glass or china containers. A thick, white glue (such as Bond's Tacky #484 or Arleen's Tacky, which can be frozen to thicken it) dries clear and is excellent for working with dried materials. I keep a tube of clear household cement (such as Duco) with my supplies and use it to reinforce petal structure. For working with woody pods and cones, I use a brown, asphalt-free linoleum paste. (The two brands I use most often are Bulldog and Permalastic.) This type of mastic is thick and great for "imbedding" heavy, woody cones in place, and, because it is brown in color, if you accidentally get some on the cones, no one will ever know. Last, but certainly not least, I keep my hot glue gun (available in hobby stores and home improvement centers) in the supply closet. If you have never tried using a hot glue gun, you are in for a real treat. They come in several sizes and price ranges. The glue comes in stick form and is easy to handle. I use hot glue for working on cones and pods, gluing foam into baskets and wooden containers, stemming flowers, attaching bows, and for many other jobs, as you will discover in subsequent chapters.

Floral Tape

This is now available in every color of the rainbow in hobby and floral-supply stores. The tape that I use most often is the stem-green color. Brownish green is also frequently called for, and white is often used in wedding work. I prefer the ½-inch-wide tape.

Floral Clay

This comes in green or white. It is used to anchor needlepoint holders in place, to join two or more containers together, or to attach a lid to the front or side of a container. I also use it to hold narrow tapers in place (sometimes at an angle) in an arrangement. (Cling is one brand name of floral clay.)

Silica Gel

Silica gel is used for drying flowers that require a desiccant, such as daffodils and roses. (This can be purchased under the name of Flower-Dri or Hazel Pearson's or Lee Ward's Silica Gel.)

Long-nosed Pliers

It is only 6 inches long, but you will soon find this to be your single most important tool. I prefer lightweight pliers that have plastic-coated handles and that are sharp wire cutters.

Needlepoint Stem Holders

The lead-based kind are the heaviest and my favorite (available at hobby stores and flower shops). I use them as stem and foam holders in shallow containers. If you already have some with plastic bases, they will work well when secured in place with floral clay. If clay is not available, melted paraffin will do.

Sand, Marbles, and Rocks

These are great for adding weight to containers that might otherwise tip over.

Rubber Bands and Twist-ties

These are for use in hanging flowers to air dry.

Wire Coat Hangers

These are for use in air drying certain kinds of flowers. I attach the flower stems to the coat hangers with bobby pins, so keep a supply of these handy in your supply closet too.

Airtight Boxes

You will need these for storing flowers that have been dried with silica gel and for storing dry silica gel.

Acrylic Sealer

You will need clear, matte-finish sealer to seal dampness from petals of dried flowers. Use glossy acrylic sealer for baskets, cones, pods, and finished pine cone projects. This is a spray-type sealer, and you should look for a brand that states on the can that the manufacturer does not use fluorocarbons (which contribute to the demise of the ozone layer). But be careful! The substitute propellant in spray cans is dangerous if you are smoking when using the spray.

Soft, Camel-hair Paintbrush

This artist's brush is used for removing silica gel film from petals and for positioning pressed materials, thus avoiding breakage.

Glycerin

Available at any drugstore, glycerin is used in preservation of ferns, leaves, and some flowers.

Books

Books are used for pressing flowers to be used in frames, on candles, for lampshade trim, and so on. The paper of these books should be of a pulp type rather than glossy. The pulp absorbs the water from the flower petals, while glossy paper holds the moisture in the flowers, causing discoloration.

Tweezers

Use the long, pointed type to place flower stems in delicate arrangements and to work with pressed flowers.

Paraffin

The type used in sealing jams and jellies is excellent. Also, used, white tapers can be broken and used. I use paraffin to seal-coat the backs of certain flowers, to weight containers, to seal kenzans in place, for dipping berries and mushrooms, sealing domes and glass jar arrangements, as a substitute for floral clay, and for making floating candles and stationary candles to add to my arrangements.

Hardware Cloth

A piece of hardware cloth bent into a rack like the one sketched on page 13 can be useful in air drying Queen Anne's lace, wild yarrow, pieces of celosia, and wire-stemmed helichrysums. A 5-foot length of mesh will give you a 3-foot surface and allow a foot on either end for "legs."

Moss

This is used in most arrangements to attractively conceal the mechanics of the design. Keep a supply of it on hand at all times.

GATHERING FILLER MATERIALS

And now comes the fun part. Pack a picnic lunch and take the children or a friend on a field trip to collect an assortment of the wild materials to be used as filler for your dried arrangements.

After a heavy dew, rain, or sprinkling by the garden hose is the wrong time to gather materials for drying. Their super-wet condition would result in loss of shape of the flowers and development of mildew. To obtain the best possible results for drying flowers, using any of the methods I will be describing for you, you must dry them as rapidly as possible. Starting with plant material picked after the morning dew has dissipated and before the afternoon sun has wilted it gives you a head start in the drying process.

Inspect the weeds, grasses, and flowers you plan to dry and pick only the ones that have just begun to open. Those already in bloom may be ready to shatter upon drying and may have been bruised or torn by the wind and rain. To dry flowers that are just opening will assure you of having fresh, perfect flowers with strong petal structure.

Because it has been established that our aim is to dry plant material as rapidly as possible, it is important to strip all leaves from the stems, thereby removing this source of moisture to the stem and flower head. I like to strip the leaves from goldenrod, Joe-Pye-weed, dock, yarrow, boneset, and similar wildlings at the site where they are picked. If you have a pair of garden gloves with you, this procedure will be easy and quick. Simply hold the stem near the flower head with one hand while you use the gloved hand to run forefinger and thumb downward along the stem. The leaves will fall where they grew (saving you clean-up time at home), and you will also save time when it comes to bunching later on. I use a garden-type insect spray on the wildlings, after removing the leaves.

To help you recognize the wildflowers, perhaps you would like to read *A Field Guide to Wildflowers* by R. T. Peterson and M. McKenny (Houghton Mifflin Co., 1974). This excellent guide covers the wildlings found in northeastern and northcentral North America. Another good book is *A Field Guide to Pacific States Wildflowers* (Houghton Mifflin Co., 1976). Another book I have enjoyed is called *How to Know the Wildflowers* (Dover Publications, Inc., 1963) by Mrs. William Starr Dana. It is a good idea to have an identification book when you go on outings to collect natural materials for drying.

Moss is a natural material important to the flower arrangement, and you should be on the lookout for it whenever you are collecting wildlings to air dry. It would be impossible to bunch moss for drying, but I have found two good ways of drying it in sheets or small clumps. I use a trowel to dig a patch of moss, being careful to leave at least an inch of soil attached to the roots. I then place the moss on crumpled newspaper which I have placed in a shoe box. The crumpled paper will allow the air to circulate around the moss, drying

Lichens grow in many shapes and colors. This fan-shaped one is quite common in the northeast. They can be found on rocks, bark, and dead tree branches.

both moss and soil. If you have a garage, you may wish to use an old window screen, suspended between sawhorses or cement blocks. If you place the moss on the screen, the air will circulate around it freely, and it should be dry in just three to four days. To keep the moss from falling apart, leave the soil on the roots of the moss until you are ready to use it in an arrangement.

Lichen is another natural material that you should be looking for on your field trips. (See figure.) To me, this is one of the most amazing plants in existence. It is a "leftover" from the age of the dinosaur and most people walk right over it and never even see it. Yet these fascinating plants of the vegetable kingdom made possible the dye industries of ancient Rome and Renaissance Florence. They are usually seen growing on rocks, bark, or dead branches on the floor of the woodlands. Some resemble small, white fans and can be picked quite easily. These are very lightweight. Others grow to be large and heavy and require digging to pry them loose from where they are growing. All lichen will dry well if you place them on a screen or on crushed newspaper in a box. You will find some truly amazing facts about this strange plant in the Spring section of this book.

Interesting tree branches and roots will make a good addition to your collection of naturals. Birch branches are delicate and lightweight. Weeping willow branches are flexible and can be reshaped. Pussy willow branches air dry perfectly and add just the right touch to most spring arrangements. The Japanese sekko, fantail, and corkscrew willows are arrangements in themselves. Each of their branches are so unusual in shape that you will frequently want to make them the highlight of your arrangement.

Seashells are not to be overlooked when collecting natural materials for dried arrangements. They can be readily found at the seashore and in children's toy boxes. You can even recruit the children to help you collect shells and driftwood while vacationing by the sea. Wired and stemmed shells add a nautical touch to arrangements made for use in a vacation home or for gift giving to men who enjoy boating or fishing.

Cones and pods are the sturdiest of the natural plant materials and are excellent for children's craft projects. They are also good items to use in occupational therapy classes and when working with senior citizens, as they are large and sturdy enough to handle without the frustration of breakage. They air dry well by placing in the sunshine outdoors. It is a good idea to spray all cones and pods with a garden-type insect spray before taking them into your home. When I have cones that are especially "sappy" and sticky to the touch, I dry them in the oven. If you have green cones, picked from the tree before they were ready to open, they also can be opened in the oven. (To oven-dry cones heat a conventional-type oven to 300°F. and then *turn it off.* Place sticky cones and those you wish to open on a cookie sheet covered with foil. Place the cones in the oven and leave them there until the oven cools completely. *Never place cones in an oven when the heat is turned on,* as the sap they contain is highly flammable.)

Nuts and acorns add wonderfully woody touches to dried arrangements if they are "cured" properly. By heating your oven to 300°F. and then turning it off, placing nuts and acorns on a foil-covered cookie sheet in the oven, and leaving them there until the oven cools, you will be assured that germination has been halted and that acorn or nut sprouts will not appear breaking through the shell to spoil your arrangement.

Berries of all kinds add a unique touch to any arrangement. The rosy-pink pepper berries are very pretty in colonial arrangements and Christmas designs. I have gathered them in Santa Barbara and Solvang, California, and also in Georgia and Florida. I dry them by hanging the branches separately to avoid their tangling. Pyracantha berries (firethorn) come in several intensities of orange, and I have good luck drying them on top of my bookcases. (Because heat rises, it is always warmer near the ceiling.) The bookcases look lovely "crowned" with pyracantha branches, and they dry with a minimum of shriveling.

Another way to dry these berries is to arrange them in a basket and place them on top of a refrigerator. The heat comes up the back and across the top of mine and, in the process, dries the berries. Also, because of the additional heat from cooking and baking, I find the berries dry rapidly in this location.

Bittersweet is protected by conservation laws in many states. If you have some growing on your property, why not pick some of the fruited branches for drying while they are still green? They will retain the fresh green coloring when dried and make an exceptional addition to any arrangement. Also, dry some when they have turned orange, hanging them separately to avoid loss of berries due to tangles.

Burning bush, spindle tree, or wahoo (depending on where you live) produces fruited branches that resemble that of the bittersweet. The seed capsules of this tree are a bright shocking pink and actually look quite artificial. They dangle from the twigs on hairlike stems, as if to decorate the woods for fall.

Strawberry bush (or hearts-a-bursting) has a reddish pink capsule concealing bright orange seeds and is often mistaken for burning bush. These fruited branches should be cut for air drying before they split open.

Rose hips of the multiflora rose and the wild rose are red and glossy and dry beautifully if you just place them on a screen or hang them on a wire coat hanger.

Jet bead berries are black and shiny and ready to use in an arrangement as soon as they are picked. They won't shrivel and have sturdy, woody stems. The jet bead bush will grow from seed rapidly and makes a fine landscape planting wherever you would like to have a bush covered with delicate white blossoms in the spring. The blossoms are almost identical to those of the mock orange bush.

Witch-hazel branches have an unusual, woody pod that remains firmly attached all through the winter. These branches look equally at home in a spring or fall arrangement and are frequently found in oriental-type designs.

Crape myrtle bushes are known for their beautiful blossoms, which air dry nicely, and for their glossy foliage. As much as I appreciate their delicate flower clusters, I look forward to gathering the seed heads in the fall. The pods resemble tiny wooden flowers and look especially pretty in fall arrangements. They will air dry on the bush and can be picked any time after turning brown for that woody look. Pick some while they are still green, and they will retain this pretty green tone which is so welcome in dried arrangements. Crape myrtle grows wild in Australia.

For delicate-appearing yet sturdy woody additions to your arrangements, be sure to collect the pods of lilac, peony, rhododendron, delphinium, and poppy.

Pittosporum seeds dry in clusters that resemble nuts. These look quite distinctive on pine cone wreaths and in other holiday decorations.

Yucca pods, rose of sharon, and jimson weed pods are all very sturdy and can be used in dried designs as "unusual flowers" for they look just like wooden flowers. The jimson weed pods resemble wooden tulips. In pine cone baskets and wreaths they can be used as finishing touches, simply glued in place on top of the completed design.

While reading about these interesting pods that are easy to dry and fun to work with, I know you have been thinking about the many plants that are growing in your garden and neighborhood that are worth checking for your pod collection. In the Fall section of this book you will be designing with woody pods and cones, making decorative items for the home that can be enjoyed all through the year, so be sure to add to your pine cone and woody pod collection whenever possible. It is always better to have a few more than you need than to run short.

Teasel is one of nature's more unusual plants and has been used in several of my designs. It is a form of thistle and grows wild in many parts of the United States and Canada. In France it is cultivated for a specific purpose: to brush or "tease" the face of soft mohair fabric. No mechanical device will perform this task. The teasel burrs are attached to large machinery rollers in rows to do this brushing. The combination of man-made heavy machinery and natural teasel burrs is a unique sight.

PLANTING FLOWERS

If you are just becoming interested in the exciting hobby of drying flowers, I have several suggestions of things you can do in the winter to get ready for spring. Dreaming your way through seed catalogs will do wonders to lift the spirit and chase the winter blues. With pad and pencil in hand, go through the catalogs and carefully select the types of flowers that will dry well in the color you will most often

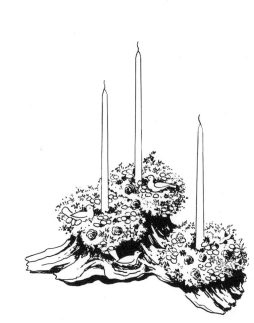

An interesting piece of driftwood, with candle holders attached, can make an unusual arrangement with just a small amount of dried materials, shells, and a few inquisitive seagull ornaments.

want to use. Refer to the list of some excellent seedsmen offering catalogs in Sources for Supplies in the back of this book, and you may
also find seed catalogs at your local library.

Measure the area of your yard that is suitable for planting.
This should be an area that receives full sun and is out of the way of
little feet. Check the Quick Reference Chart in the back of the book for
flowers that dry well and then look for those seeds in the catalogs.
The flowers that will produce blooms every year (perennials), such as
yarrow, candytuft, cornflowers, and roses, to name just a few, should
be planted where they will not have to be disturbed. Also their size
must be considered. Some varieties of yarrow will grow 4 feet high so
you certainly would not want to plant them as a border to your garden. Candytuft grows close to the ground, looks lacy white and lovely
in a rock garden, and can also be used as a border. The cornflower or
bachelor button will produce well for two years, and also grows tall.
Rose bushes should be separated by at least 2 feet in all directions so
they will have good air circulation around them, thus avoiding mildew, and so you will be able to cut the roses from all sides.

The seed catalogs will tell you if the seeds you are interested in
are annuals or perennials and how high they will grow under ideal
conditions. Some of the easy-to-grow-and-dry everlastings you may
want to try are the dwarf variety of helichrysum, which grows to a
height of 15 inches. The tall variety of helichrysum will grow to 30
inches and will require staking for support. The globe amaranth, an
attractive ball-shaped flower similar in appearance to clover, will
reward you with blooms from midsummer until frost. It will grow in
hot, dry locations and the flowers are very long-lasting when dried.
The more flowers you pick while the plant is in bloom, the more
flowers will be produced. George Washington is credited with bringing the first globe amaranths to America, and they are still planted
annually in the garden at Mount Vernon. Celosia of the floradale or
prairie-fire varieties are excellent for drying and retain a vivid color.
Of the many varieties of zinnia that dry well, my favorites are the cut-
and-come-again, Persian carpet, and green envy. Larkspur in blue,
white, or pink dry well and will give you a spike-type of material for
your arrangements. The marigold, known also as the friendship
flower, grows easily and blooms in all fifty of the United States. The
marigold is native to America, and the golden climax, primrose, yellow nugget, and red and gold hybrids dry best for me. If you have
some other varieties growing in your garden, try drying them. You
may be pleasantly surprised.

Remembering that you will be supplementing the flowers you
dry from the garden with wildlings, the materials gathered in the
meadows and woodlands, this may be all the garden you care to
plant in the spring. Some "fillers," such as baby's breath, German
statice, and gypsy broom bloom, are better to purchase as needed;
they take over the garden space better used for prettier flowers.

After you have decided which flowers you would like to plant
next spring and have planned the space where they will grow, order

*Clothesline or wire strung between
attic rafters is ideal for hanging
bunched materials for drying. Dark,
warm, and well-ventilated attics are
best to preserve natural colors. Bright
sun can fade colors, and lack of
ventilation can cause mildew.*

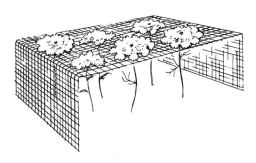

A hardware-cloth rack, for drying materials that dry best in an upright position, keeps the heads of each flower separated during the process and results in better shapes.

Hanging individual flowers, such as ageratum, tiger lilies, cornflowers, delphinium, blue sage, and bridal wreath, on a coat hanger will allow them to dry with a maximum of air circulation and a minimum of damage due to tangling. The bobby pins act as clamps, tightening as the stems dehydrate and keeping the flowers from falling.

the seeds so there will be no delay in planting them once all danger of frost has passed.

METHODS OF PRESERVING FLOWERS

Considering the high cost of fresh flowers and our short growing season for garden flowers, you will receive tremendous satisfaction from preserving seasonal flowers that can be enjoyed all through the year. There are six methods of preserving flowers in this section, and, with any one of them, your arrangements will look as though they are "minutes fresh" from the garden years after you have assembled them.

Method 1 Air Drying

This is undoubtedly the easiest method of drying the filler material that you gathered. Unfortunately, not all flowers can be handled in this manner. The everlasting flowers, such as statice, globe amaranth, helichrysum, sea lavender, and ammobium, respond best to this method of drying, as they are already papery dry when growing in your garden. It is merely a matter of drying their stems.

Other plant materials you will enjoy air drying are the weeds, grasses, pods, and cones.

Upon returning from a field trip, it is important to bunch and hang your harvest as soon as possible, so that the air can begin circulating around them, drying them with the best color and form. For best results, select an area free of dampness, preferably with air circulation, such as an attic. In an apartment, a utility closet containing a hot water heater will suffice. String a wire or clothesline to hang fresh materials. (See figure.) When bunching the flowers, do not cram too many stems into the same bunch. This will not only crush and misshape some of your flower heads but will prolong the drying process and possibly cause some spoiling of your "treasures" by mildew. You will be able to gauge how many stems to include in a bunch by looking at the flower end of the stems while they are bunched in your hand. If the flower heads seem dense and compacted, remove several stems from the bunch and rearrange flower heads so they are separate from each other. To hold the bunches together for hanging, I use rubber bands affixed to the stems about 2 inches from the stem ends. By placing the rubber band near the end of the stems, you allow the bunch to fan out at the flower end, thus allowing for better circulation of air around the flowers. As the stems dry and shrink, the rubber band will tighten, holding the bunch together. When twine or wire is used for bunching, as the stems shrink they begin falling from the bunch.

To hang your bunches of flowers you will need some *S*-shaped hooks. These are easily made from 3-inch lengths of stem wire or from twist-ties bent into the shape of an *S*. Hook the lower part of the *S* under the rubber band and hang the bunch by the top part of the hook. When hanging flowers to dry, be sure to leave plenty of space between each bunch to encourage free flow of air. If you are experiencing humid weather, you may wish to place a circulating fan and portable heater or dehumidifier in the drying room. To assure brightness of color, keep the drying area as dark as possible without restricting airflow.

The time involved in drying your flowers by this natural method will vary according to the part of the country in which you reside, the type of weather you are having, and the type of flowers with which you are working. If you are drying flowers during a hot, dry spell, they should be ready for use in a week or two. If you had a rainy period for several days prior to picking the flowers, or if it rains for several days after you hang your bunches for drying, it may take three weeks or longer before the material dries thoroughly.

It is very important that you not store your material until you are certain it is completely dry, as mildew could result. You will know when it is dry by bending a stem. If the stem snaps, it is dry. If the stem bends, there is still moisture in it, and you had better wait a little longer to complete drying. See the Quick Reference Chart in the back of the book for specifics.

Once the bunched flowers are dry, remove them from the drying area, so they will not reabsorb moisture from the flowers you will be drying next. I have found shoe boxes to be excellent storage containers, because they are deep, uniform in size, long enough (seldom will you have need for longer stems), and easily stackable.

To properly store your dried material, line a shoe box with a piece of tissue paper or waxed paper. Remove the rubber bands from the bunched flowers and save them for your next bunching session. Break stems to a length that will fit into the shoe box without touching ends of the box. Place some flower heads at one end of the box and some at the opposite end. Place a sheet of tissue paper between each layer to prevent tangling. Do not pack too many to a box or you will lose quality by flattening or breaking some of your flowers. When the box is filled and ready to store, position lid in place and seal it on with masking tape, running tape around entire edge of lid to seal out moisture. The masking tape is easily removed when you are ready to work with the flowers and will not tear the box. On the end of the box place a label that will tell you the name and color of the flower in the box and the date stored. You may be able to store your shoe box treasury on the shelf nearest the ceiling in a coat closet where there may be existing waste space. Do not store the boxes in the basement or in other locations where they may pick up moisture.

Not all plant material responds well to identical treatment. The Quick Reference Chart in the back of the book will show you at a glance which method is preferable.

Have you been wondering which flowers will respond best to air drying? It is always exciting to experiment, but, generally speaking, the following flowers (see figures) will give you that heady feeling of success on your very first try:

Acacia *(Decurens dealbata)*

Ageratum *(Eupatorium coelestinum)*

Baby's breath *(Gypsophila)*

Bachelor button *(Centaurea cyanus)*

Blue sage *(Salvia farinacea)*

China asters *(Callistephus chinensis)*

Beauty-berry *(Callicarpa purpurea)*

Boneset *(Eupatorium)*

Chinese lanterns *(Physallis alkekengi)*

Bells of Ireland *(Molucella laevis)*

Cattails *(Typha)*

Chives, leeks, ornamental onions
(Allium)

Cockscomb, crested (*Celosia cristata*)

Dock (*Rumex crispus*)

Globe thistle (*Echinops*)

Cockscomb, plumed (*Celosia agrentea*)

Dusty miller (*Artemesia*)

Grasses, ornamental (*Briza maxima, Lagurus*)

Delphinium (*Delphinium elatum*)

Globe amaranth (*Gomphrena globosa*)

Heal-all, self-heal (*Prunella vulgaris*)

Heather *(Calluna vulgaris)*

Ironweed *(Veronia noveboracensis)*

Lavender *(Lavandula)*

Helichrysums *(Helichrysum bracteatum)*

Joe-Pye-weed *(Eupatorium maculatum)*

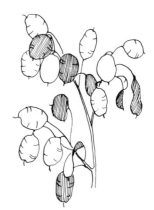

Lunaria, honesty, or silver dollar
(Lunaria annua)

Hydrangea *(Hydrangea macrophylla)*

Larkspur *(Delphinium)*

Milkweed *(Asclepias syriaca)*

Mint flowers
(Mentha arvensis, spicata, or piperita)

Pennycress *(Thlaspi arvense)*

Poke berries *(Phytolacca americana)*

Mullein *(Verbascum thapsus)*

Pepper berries, Brazilian pepper
(Terebinthifolius)

Pussy-toes *(Antennaria)*

Pearly everlasting
(Anaphalis margaritacea)

Peppergrass *(Lepidium virginicum)*

Queen Anne's lace *(Daucus carota)*

Rabbit-foot clover *(Trifolium arvense)*

Statice *(Limonium sinuatum)*

Xeranthemum *(Xeranthemum annum)*

Rhodanthe *(Helipterum manglesii)*

Tansy *(Tanacetum vulgare)*

Yarrow, hybrid *(Achillea)*

Sea lavender *(Limonium latifolium)*

Teasel *(Dipsacus sylvestris)*

Yarrow, wild *(Achillea millefolium)*

I am sure you have found some flowers on this list that are native to your area. There are many more pods, leaves, and flowers that are easy to dry, and they will be talked about in the seasonal chapters that follow.

Method 2   Conventional Use of Silica Gel

I have described the rather simple procedures of air drying flowers, weeds, grasses and woody pods, cones, lichen, moss, and acorns. These materials are wonderful to work with when creating fall arrangements and other informal designs. The use of silica gel in preserving flowers takes a little more patience, but the results are exhilarating. The flowers you would dry in silica gel are generally not the same ones that would dry well by hanging. A few flowers will dry well by either method and they are noted in the Quick Reference Chart in the back of this book.

The types of flowers that require silica gel for best preservation are listed below:

Ajuga	Freesia	Queen Anne's lace
Anemones	Grape Hyacinths	Roses
Azaleas	Lily of the Valley	Snapdragons
Crocus	Marigolds	Stokesias
Daffodils	Pansies	Tulips
Daisies	Passionflowers	Zinnias
Dogwood	Peonies	

All of these flowers have fleshy stems and very delicate petals. Because they contain so much water, if you were to air dry them, it would take many weeks, during which time they would become limp, losing both their color and shape. The plant materials that air dry best are the ones that are strawlike or almost dry when you pick them. So, to dry these more delicate flowers in silica gel (which is a desiccant) the trick is to dehydrate the blooms rapidly enough to preserve both their vibrant, natural colors and their intricate shapes.

When it is necessary to maintain absolute dryness, silica gel has been used commercially for many years. The military uses it in packing foods, film, and ammunition for shipment to tropical areas. You may have found a packet of it in your bag of potato chips or a vitamin capsule bottle. (It is put in to absorb moisture.) This grade of silica gel is too coarse for use in drying flowers as the rough crystals would cause unsightly marks on the petals. The silica gel that is manufactured expressly for use in preserving flowers is a sandy-type agent, almost powdery in texture. In fact, it is an ingredient of most toothpastes. Silica gel is not a jellylike substance but is white in color, resembling fine beach sand and lighter in weight than sandbox sand. It contains bright blue crystals of cobalt chloride which act as moisture indicators. As the silica gel begins to absorb moisture from the flowers embedded in it, the cobalt chloride crystals will indicate this by turning light blue and then pink. When the silica gel has absorbed up to 40 percent of its own weight in moisture, it will still feel powdery dry to the touch, but will no longer be effective in removing moisture from flowers. At this point, the cobalt chloride crystals will indicate this state of supersaturation by turning white. The silica gel must then be reactivated before it can be successfully used again.

Reactivation can be accomplished by simply placing the silica gel in a shallow, oven-proof dish (such as a lasagna casserole) and putting the dish in the oven at 250°F. for half an hour or until the cobalt chloride crystals return to their original bright blue color. At this point, the silica gel is ready to be used again or to be stored in airtight containers for cooling until needed. As silica gel will absorb moisture from the air as well as from flowers buried in it, it is best to keep it covered at all times.

Incidentally, silica gel is not toxic if ingested, but, as with all powdery substances, it is best not to inhale it.

Hobby and craft stores sell silica gel under various brand names (Flower-Dri is one and Hazel Pearson is another. Lee Wards also packages it.) Also, some garden centers and florists handle this product. A four-pound container costs about nine dollars (as of the writing of this book), but considering that silica gel is reusable indefinitely, this is quite a bargain.

To dry flowers and foliage with silica gel, it is necessary to pick the flowers when they have just opened. This assures you of preserving a perfect flower that has not been damaged by wind or rain. Also, petal structure is strongest at this point of development and thus the flower can withstand the weight of the silica gel better. It is imperative that the blooms be absolutely dry. If dew or other moisture is on the petals at the time you cover the flower with silica gel, the desiccant will stick to the petals. In trying to remove the powdery residue once the flower is dried, you may ruin the entire flower. So, start with a freshly opened flower picked when the morning dew has disappeared and before the afternoon sun has had a chance to wilt the bloom.

It is a good idea to begin with a daisy-type flower, (any flower that has one circle of petals). Leave a 2-inch stem on each flower.

In preparation for using silica gel, place it in a casserole dish, then place the casserole in a conventional gas or electric oven at 250°F. for thirty minutes to make sure it is dry. (If you are using a microwave oven, heat the silica gel for two minutes on "high.") The cobalt chloride moisture-indicator crystals in the silica gel will turn bright blue when the desiccant is ready to use.

When it is flecked with blue crystals, set the casserole aside to cool. Cover it with plastic food wrap to prevent moisture in the air from being absorbed by the cooling gel. If condensation appears on the plastic cover, remove it and return the silica gel to the oven to complete drying.

When the silica gel has dried thoroughly and is cool, place it in a tin cake box with a tight-fitting lid or in a plastic food storage container with a lid that will seal out the moisture.

Flowers dried in silica gel generally require two to five days for drying. If you were to use sand or similar materials, it would take from three to six *weeks*.

Since the flowers you will be drying will have retained varying amounts of water while growing, it is impossible to come up with a specific formula of drying periods. The Quick Reference Chart at the back of this book provides good guidelines for timing that usually work well for me. Much depends, however, upon the type of flower you are drying, the size of the bloom, how much moisture it contains, and other variables.

A zinnia or any flower with one circle of petals is a good choice to start with. Using an airtight container, place an inch of dry silica gel on the bottom. If the container will hold six flowers with a 3-inch space between each, place a teaspoon of silica gel where each of the six flowers will be placed to dry. These little mounds of silica gel will support the flowers so that they will not dry flat. Place one flower, face down, over each mound. (See figure.)

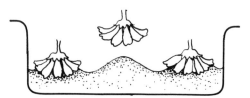

The little mounds of silica gel preserve the shape of these zinnias so that they will not flatten under the weight of the desiccant.

Using a tablespoon, spoon the silica gel against the side of the container, away from the flowers, so that it slides down the side of the container and under each petal of each flower without causing undue weight on the flower. (See figure.) Continue pouring the gel against the container's sides until the flowers are totally covered. When placing several flowers in the same container for drying at the same time, be sure to separate them well, so that moisture does not seep from one flower to another. When the flowers are completely covered with silica gel, seal the airtight container with the lid and set it aside.

It is a good idea to date the container to help you remember when to check for dryness. When drying several flowers in the same container, it is also a good idea to make sure that they are the same type of flower. If they are daisy-type flowers, they will all be dry at the same time. But if, for instance, you have a daisy-type flower with a rose and a peony in the same drying container, they will *not* be dry in the same period of time. The additional handling of the flowers while testing for dryness could cause breakage of the petals.

Cover the flower by spooning silica gel down the container's sides.

To determine if the flowers are dry, run your finger through the silica gel near the outer edge of the container, where you are sure of not "bumping" the flowers, or tilt the container. As the silica gel filters away from the flowers and the petal tips are exposed, *gently* feel them. They should feel crisp and papery dry. If they are still soft, re-cover them and let them stand a while longer. When you are sure the flowers are dry, gently pour the gel from the container until enough of the flowers are uncovered to allow you to pick them up by the stem. (See figure.)

To store the dried flowers until you have enough of them to begin an arrangement or project, place them face up in an airtight container of dry builder's sand. The container should have about 2 inches of sand in it, just enough to cushion the flowers and hold them

Slowly pour the silica gel from the container until enough flowers are uncovered to allow for picking them up by their stem ends.

in an upright position. (See figure.)

Before reusing the silica gel, take time to heat it to make sure it is thoroughly dry. The warmed gel will also hasten the drying time of the flowers you are about to work with.

To dry flowers that have many petals, such as marigolds and roses, place them in the silica gel face up. Using a tablespoon, spoon the silica gel against the side of the container, so that it slides down the side of the container and around each of the flowers, bracing them so they do not fall over and letting the crystals seep between each layer of petals. When they are completely covered with silica gel, place the airtight lid on the container, mark the date on it, and set it aside. Refer to the Quick Reference Chart at the back of this book for the correct drying time.

To determine if the flowers are dry, use the same method described for testing single petal flowers. When you are certain of their dryness, store them in an airtight container of oven-dried builder's sand until you are ready to use them.

Imagine how exciting it is going to be when you have dried a nice assortment of flowers from which you can now pick and choose when you are ready to make an arrangement for your home or for a friend.

Method 3   Preheated Silica Gel

In Method 2 I explained flower preservation via the conventional silica gel method. Because I dry a great many flowers for use at speaking engagements and in classes, I prefer to heat my silica gel first. By so doing, I obtain a maximum number of dry flowers in a minimum amount of time, because flowers dry faster in preheated silica gel.

Preheat the silica gel by placing it in a glass oven-proof dish and heating it, uncovered, at 250°F. in a conventional oven for ten to fifteen minutes.

Remove silica gel from the oven and place one inch of the warm gel in the bottom of an airtight container. If your container is the size that will hold three or four flowers at one time, place a teaspoon of silica gel for each flower to be dried, forming three or four mounds around the edge of the container. Place one flower face down over each mound. The mound will keep the flower from drying completely flat.

Using a tablespoon, slowly sift the desiccant against the side of the container so that it slides down the side of the container and under each petal. Continue pouring silica gel against the container's side until all of the flowers are covered. Usually ½ inch of silica gel is enough to cover a circle-type flower.

Place the lid on the container and seal it. Date it so that you will know when to check for dryness. Refer to the Quick Reference Chart at the back of this book for suggested drying times for various flowers.

Flowers stored in dry builder's sand in an airtight container will retain their natural shape.

Method 4   Silica Gel and the Microwave Oven

Because your object is to dry flowers as fast as possible in order to retain their natural color and form, the microwave oven can be a veritable "magic wand." A flower that might take five days to dry with the conventional silica gel method or three days to dry using preheated silica gel will dry in just one minute in the microwave.

One of the advantages of drying flowers with such speed is that you will be able to accumulate an assortment of blooms for an arrangement in a relatively short time. Another advantage is that you will be able to dry many flowers while they are at the peak of their growing season. For instance, if you are drying roses and it takes five days to determine if they have dried well, it may be too late to try again, as the roses may no longer be in bloom. But, if you dry a rose the microwave method, you will know within twenty minutes if you have successfully preserved that rose. If for any reason the rose is less than perfect, you may immediately cut another rose from the bush and try again.

In drying flowers by Method 2 or 3, you may dry three or four flowers of the same kind in the same container simultaneously, providing the container is large enough to allow at least 3 inches between each flower. This prevents seepage of moisture from one flower to another. When drying flowers in the microwave, it is best to dry only one flower at a time. One reason for this is that the less heat the flowers are subjected to, the better color will result. The more flowers placed in the microwave oven at the same time, the longer amount of time they will have to be in the oven. The increased amount of time could cause a severe color loss. The exception to this rule is the pansy. Because the petals of pansies are so thin and fragile, I dry three of these flowers simultaneously, in separate cups, for just one minute.

Another advantage to drying a single flower at a time is that you will be able to correct the timing, if necessary, without losing more than one flower. If you have dried five or six roses and discover your heat was too high, you may not have many roses left in your garden with which to start over. Generally, I will time a multipetaled flower like the rose for two minutes in the microwave on high heat. Once removed from the oven, I let it remain undisturbed for twenty to thirty minutes. At that point, I check for crispness of the petal tips by gently pouring the silica gel from the cup until the tips are exposed. If they feel papery dry, I continue pouring the gel from the cup until I can easily pick up the flower by the stem. If the rose has good color and shape and the petals are holding together well, I can then continue drying other roses for the same timing. If the test rose has become rather beige in color, I know that (a) the rose was past its prime when dried or had been exposed to too much rain, or (b) the rose contained less moisture than normal, due to lack of rain, and thus will have to be dried at half the heat used. I will then dry the next rose for one minute only, let it remain outside the oven for twenty to thirty minutes and then check for quality of color and petal crispness. Timing can be cut in half again, if you are still not pleased with the color or if you just wish to experiment. I seldom have to cut the timing back more than once.

Another advantage of drying flowers in the microwave oven is that you will not need to purchase a great deal of silica gel. When you are using Method 2 or 3, your silica gel is tied up for many days at a time, which prevents you from using it to dry additional flowers. When you are preserving flowers in the microwave oven, you are able to reuse the silica gel usually within the hour.

For your first attempt at using the microwave method of preserving flowers, I recommend drying a zinnia or daisy-type flower. These flowers with one circle of petals are sturdy and easy to work with, and they practically assure success with your very first try. For containers, I prefer plastic or glass measuring cups, oven-proof custard cups, or Corelle open-handle coffee cups. (*Metal containers must never be used in a microwave oven.*) To begin, preheat the silica gel in the microwave oven until the cobalt chloride crystals turn blue (about one minute). Select a cup at least 2½ inches taller than the flower you are drying. Place one inch of the warm silica gel in the bottom of the cup. Add a teaspoon of silica gel in the center, forming a small mound. Position the flower face down, on the mound. The mound will support the flower, allowing it to dry in a natural cup shape rather than flat. (See the figure on page 22.)

Slowly pour spoonfuls of gel against the sides of the cup, turning and tilting the cup as you pour. The silica gel will slide down the cup sides and under each petal without causing undue weight on the flower. Continue adding silica gel until the entire flower is covered, leaving at least 2 inches from the top of the silica gel to the top of the container, so none of the gel will pop out during drying.

Continual experimentation is the secret to determining the exact length of time for drying flowers in the microwave oven, since even the same species can differ in moisture content on different days.

Method 5 The Microwave Oven Alone

Something that is noticeably missing from the dried arrangements frequently seen in shops is green foliage. Some dried arrangements even resemble small bushes, where the designer has overcompensated for the lack of leaves by using too much filler. To avoid this lack-luster appearance in your arrangements, spend a little time drying a nice collection of leaves to work with. Florists buy large amounts of sturdy commercial fillers. You, on the other hand, can dry beautiful, more fragile green foliage for use in your individual arrangements.

If you do not own a microwave oven, perhaps a friend will share with you. The procedure is simple, fast, and clean. It requires only the microwave oven, the leaves, and a supply of paper napkins. (See figure.)

In my microwave oven I have successfully dried strawberry leaves, maidenhair fern, and the foliage of ajuga, lily of the valley,

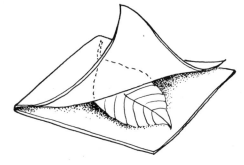

One, two, or three leaves may be placed in a paper napkin and dried simultaneously in a microwave oven, resulting in perfect color retention.

English ivy, *Vinca minor*, hosta, mock orange, jet bead, day lily, dumb cane, leatherleaf viburnum, and forsythia. These leaves all held their natural green coloring, and the lily of the valley and hosta leaves retained their lovely sheen. The photograph of my arrangement on the stained-glass mirror (see color plates) shows how lily of the valley leaves actually make the dried arrangement look like a fresh bouquet. *Vinca minor* leaves were used in the arrangement on page 52 and add a light, delicate finishing touch to that design.

Fall leaves dry with all their brilliant coloring and truly make a fall arrangement special.

To dry leaves in your microwave oven place a leaf or two on a paper napkin half. Fold the other half of the napkin over the leaves to completely cover them. Place an oven-proof custard cup, upside down, over the napkin to keep the leaves from curling, and set your oven for two minutes. When the two minutes are up, remove the custard cup from the napkin and wipe the interior of the cup dry. If leaves feel stiff and dry, they need not be returned to the oven. If they are almost dry, they may be placed on a paper towel overnight, and they will be dry by morning. If they are really quite damp, they must be returned to the microwave oven for another minute. Seldom will you have to dry a leaf for more than three minutes. It is a good idea to let leaves that are only slightly damp remain out of the oven for five minutes or so (in the same manner you would set a baked potato aside to finish cooking, once removed from the oven).

If your leaves look too dried when removed from the oven, cut the oven time in half for the next leaves of similar type and size. This may produce a more pleasing texture. Over-dried leaves look rough and shriveled. By drying most of my leaves for just two minutes, on "high," I obtain excellent color and texture.

To add shape to a leaf remove it from the oven while still slightly damp and pliable, place it on a dry napkin, and place a "hot dog shaped" roll of waxed paper under the center of the leaf. I let it dry over night covered with another dry napkin.

Some flowers can also be dried using the microwave oven alone. For example, I have dried sweet everlasting and pearly everlasting flowers in my microwave oven, without the use of silica gel. To dry these wildlings, place them on a paper napkin in the microwave oven and turn the heat indicator to one minute on "high." If they are not dry at that point, return them to the oven for another minute. As with foods prepared in a microwave oven, it is necessary to let the flowers remain out of the oven for five minutes, while the internal heat continues to dry them. When the five minutes have lapsed, if they require further drying, return them to the oven for another minute.

I have discovered a marvelous method of preserving the newer, delicate, colored varieties of celosia in all their true shades of palest pink, pastel yellow, fiery orange, and rose-tinted orange. This is a great satisfaction because until now, the newer colors have been exciting to see in the garden, but have totally lost their vibrancy in drying.

These newer types of cockscomb form heavy, quite densely compacted heads and so must be broken into floret pieces, 1 to 2 inches each, in order to be dried in the microwave oven. Four or five of these pieces can be placed on a paper napkin half and covered with the other half of the napkin, placed in the microwave oven on "high" for two minutes. The result: miracles! Your celosia florets, only minutes from the garden, will be preserved in all their brilliant jewellike colors and ready to be used in an arrangement!

The florets may be glued together to form flower heads the size of a silver dollar or larger, or stemmed and used in their present size and shape. The small florets may also be used in a completed design, simply glued to the filler without stemming.

The beautiful, feathery looking plumed celosia flowers also dry well in the microwave oven (on a paper napkin, on "high," for two minutes). The smaller, lightweight plumes will require only one minute. The colors will be almost true and the plume-like shape of the flower can be restored by gently shaking it or by running your finger over the edge of the bloom. The bloom flattens some while drying.

Although blue sage responds well to air drying and preservation in silica gel, the most rapid method I have discovered is the "paper napkin, microwave oven" way.

You can place four or five stems of blue sage on a paper napkin half, cover them with the other half of the napkin, and dry them for four minutes on "high." The flowers will then be ready to use in an arrangement or to store for future use, and the color preserved will be absolutely perfect.

Globe amaranths air dry to perfection. However, if you find it necessary to dry some of these flowers rapidly for immediate use, they will dry in the microwave oven, on a paper napkin, with no loss of color, in just two minutes.

Leave a 5-inch stem on the globe amaranths when drying in the microwave oven, to avoid having to wire-stem them. The stems will dry well.

The queen of everlasting flowers, helichrysum, air dries well on wire stems, in an upright position. If it becomes necessary to dry some of these flowers rapidly for immediate use, they will respond well to drying on a paper napkin in the microwave oven. Upon removing them from the two-minute drying period in the oven, immediately wire-stem them. If the flower head hardens, the wire stem will not be able to penetrate. It will then be necessary to use hot glue to attach the wire stems.

Method 6   Glycerin

One of the easiest ways to enrich your home with natural beauty is through the use of foliage. As you saw in Method 5, you can dry green leaves in the microwave oven. Another method is to glycerinize them.

Those of us who were not blessed with a "green thumb" agonize as our lovely houseplants cease to thrive. However, there are two inexpensive ways in which even "nonplant people" can enjoy greenery in their homes throughout the year. One method is to cut branches of evergreens, crush their woody stems with a hammer, 2 to 3 inches from the end of the stem, and arrange them in an attractive vase. What could be easier? Magnolia, pittosporum, eucalyptus, shallon (lemon leaf), viburnum, and rhododendron leaves look exceptionally beautiful when displayed this way. If the water is freshened every three or four days, the foliage will remain attractive for months. A piece of charcoal added to the water will keep it sweet and discourage algae from forming.

Another method of enjoying leaves in your home throughout the year is to preserve some for this purpose. There are several ways of doing this, but I have found three methods that yield excellent results and that are especially easy. One is the use of glycerin, a wetting agent, found in most drugstores. Another is accomplished by using a microwave oven and a paper napkin. Pressing whole branches of leaves is the third method. For the glycerin method, read on.

Leaves preserved in glycerin remain pliable, leatherlike, and can be used with dried materials or in fresh arrangements with water. Some leaves change their color to a darker green, and some become a chocolate brown or bronze color. The red maple and sumac leaves become more of a burgundy. In the northeast United States, the best time of year to process leaves in glycerin is between June and September. By June the sap has hardened and by September the sap is still "up." Young leaves processed before June are so weak and thin that they do not absorb the glycerin solution well and become extremely droopy. Leaves that are processed once the sap "goes down" are too brittle to process well. Heavier leaves, such as magnolia, viburnum, rhododendron, pittosporum, and leaves of similar thickness, seem to accept glycerin best. Since it is always fun to experiment, please do try other types of leaves.

To glycerinize foliage you will need a selection of attractive leaves that are not torn or misshapen (these should be gathered following a dry spell), a meatloaf casserole dish (or similar size container) of glass or plastic, a bottle of glycerin from the drugstore, newspapers to cover your work area, and a clean soft, damp cloth. If you only plan to preserve a small number of leaves, a small bottle of glycerin will do. If you would like to preserve enough leaves to make an interesting arrangement, start with the largest bottle you can obtain. This is usually a 4-ounce bottle and costs about $1.50 (at the time of this writing).

Begin by covering the work area with newspapers. Then wipe leaves to be processed with a damp cloth to remove dust. Do not rinse them under the faucet, as they will absorb water, which will slow their absorption of the glycerin solution.

Pour the entire contents of the bottle of glycerin into the casserole or plastic container. Fill the bottle with warm water twice and pour the water into the glycerin and stir. Your solution will then be 1:2, or one part glycerin to two parts water. One by one, add the leaves to the solution, making sure they are being evenly coated with the emollient and no air bubbles are trapped between the leaves. There should be enough space between the leaves so that they will be able to float when you tip the end of the container.

Cover the container with a lid or foil and date it. Store it on a shelf, and every three or four days, "rock the container" so that the solution will circulate around the leaves. If the leaves were picked following a rainy period, it will take longer for them to absorb the glycerin solution. If the leaves were picked after a dry spell, they will be very thirsty and will absorb the solution rapidly. The process may take from one to three weeks.

You will be able to tell when the leaves are ready to be removed from the solution by their even coloring. When you first check the leaves, they will look "spotty," as though they had been splashed with oil. When the spots disappear and the leaf coloring is even, the process has been completed. Remove the leaves to a pad of newspapers, first draining the excess solution from each leaf to save as much as possible. Place several leaves on the newspaper, none touching, covering them with about five sheets of newspaper before adding the next layer of leaves to dry. Continue this layering until all the leaves are between sheets of newspaper, able to drain dry for a week or two without the moisture seeping into the next layer of leaves. (A tabloid-size newspaper is easiest to handle for this "drying off" procedure, and, because of its size, I usually slip it under a bed, out of the way.) When the leaves have dried, wipe them with a soft tissue and store them in a shoe box, with tissue between the layers, for future use.

Your glycerin solution will probably have changed from crystal clear to a brownish color. This will *not* affect your using it indefinitely. Store it in a jar until you need it again. Should a mildew-type coating appear on the top of the solution, remove it by running a paper towel over it to absorb the spores, before reusing the solution.

Individual leaves preserved in glycerin can be used in dried flower arrangements and wreaths, to add interest to a fresh flower arrangement, or to place in a circle around a punch bowl. As a fast and easy Christmas centerpiece, glycerinized magnolia leaves are often used on a dining room table, circling an epergne of fruits, nuts, and candies. (See figure.) Shiny red apples placed on each leaf give the appearance of a Christmas wreath, and your guests can eat them for dessert! Sprigs of fresh evergreens tucked between the apples add the pefect holiday aroma.

To extend the length of the stem of a preserved leaf, follow the sketches detailing stemming of flowers. (See figures.) If your leaf needs support, run the wire stem halfway up the back of the leaf and glue it in place with just a few dots of thick white glue (such as Tacky, Velverette, or Dip 'N Dab). Let glue dry thoroughly before you proceed with taping the rest of the wire stem. (See figure.)

If you are planning to make a boughpot of glycerinized leaves for your fireplace or foyer, you may wish to preserve them while they are still attached to their branches. This method requires that you

This is the easiest and fastest Christmas or Hanukkah centerpiece you could make. It merely requires placing fresh fruit and greenery on glycerinized magnolia leaves all around an epergne on which sweet meats, fruits, and nuts have been arranged. This type of arrangement is used today, in Williamsburg, Virginia, during the Christmas season and was a favorite of the colonists.

use branches no more than 2 feet (0.6m) in length, and hammer-crush the tips of the stems about 2 to 3 inches to increase their absorption of the glycerin solution. Place the glycerin solution in an attractive vase or crock, add the branches of leaves, and place the arrangement in a dry area away from sunlight to enjoy it while they are being preserved. When using this method of branch preservation, it is necessary to wipe the uppermost leaves, back and front, with the glycerin solution. This prevents those leaves from drying out and shriveling while waiting for the solution to reach them. It is *imperative* when glycerinizing an entire branch that you cut that branch from the bush or tree *after several days of hot, dry weather.*

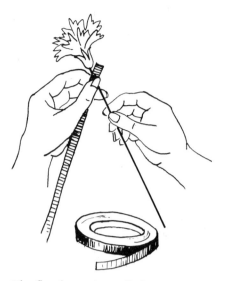

The floral tape is applied to a wire stem. Notice how the tape end is placed at an angle.

(To press the colorful leaves of fall or other branches of attractive foliage between sheets of newspaper, place a small area rug over the paper pile for weight. Pressing is an inexpensive way of obtaining a great many leaves for an arrangement rapidly. Again, because of the size of this project I slide it under the bed for several weeks, while drying. Leaves processed in this manner will not be as versatile as those preserved in glycerin, as they will be quite brittle. However, they will add a lovely touch to your fall arrangements and will surely last the season.)

Very few flowers respond well to glycerinizing, as this treatment causes flowers to become limp and lose their shape. However, some flowers are much improved by this wetting agent. Statice, for example, becomes less brittle and easier to work with; honesty pod hulls peel without damage to the pearly centers; and baby's breath lasts much longer than untreated material.

Statice *(Limonium sinuatum)* comes in luscious shades of blue, lavender, yellow, apricot, rose, white, and purple. It air dries quite well, and this is the method of drying most frequently used. It also accepts a glycerin-and-water solution which softens the papery flower heads and deepens the colors. Glycerinized flowers are not as brittle as the air-dried ones and for this reason are longer lasting and easier to work with.

If you would like to glycerinize some statice, cut the fresh stems on an angle and insert them into a glass jar containing one part glycerin and two parts warm water. The shorter the stem, the less time it will take for the solution to reach the flower heads. The process is complete when the flowers are soft to the touch. Hang them upside down for several days to dry before using.

Honesty *(Lunaria)*, sometimes called the money plant or silver dollar plant, also absorbs a glycerin solution well. The outer shells of the pods will be easier to remove if you first let the stems absorb this treatment.

Baby's breath *(Gypsophela)* air dries well, but because of its tangled nature, much of it is lost in trying to separate it once it is dry. Glycerinized baby's breath becomes a creamy ivory, rather than a snowy white, and being less brittle separates more easily than when air dried. You may purchase "preserved *Gypsophela*" in bunches, or, if you prefer to do your own, cut the stems to 6 to 8 inches and submerge them in the glycerin-and-water solution until they become

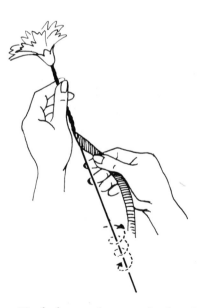

Pinch the tape between the thumb and index finger, while twirling the stem and pulling on the tape with the opposite hand, simultaneously.

evenly colored. This usually only takes a day or two. Hang, to dry thoroughly, before using.

PRESSING FLOWERS

Preserving flowers and leaves by pressing them to remove the moisture is not a new idea. It goes all the way back to the 1500s to a man named Luca Ghini in the town of Pisa in Italy. Since that time sentimentalists have pressed a flower from a loved one's wedding or funeral between the pages of the family Bible or other heavy book. Those flowers soon lost their beautiful color and only the memories remained.

Today we know a lot more about pressing flowers for better color retention. Following are the three methods I feel produce the best results.

If you do not have silica gel or a microwave oven, you can still achieve excellent results pressing blooms. Open a pressing book (one with pulp-type paper) to about ten pages from the back and place a facial tissue on that page. Place four or five blossoms on the tissue, if they are about the size of a buttercup. If they are larger, two or three may be all you should fit on a page to be certain they do not overlap or touch each other. (The idea is to have good separation between each flower so moisture does not seep from one flower to another.)

Be sure to press some flowers fully open, some side views, and some just in bud. Also press some leaves and stems to use when reconstructing the flowers in a flower print or other project.

When the first page is filled, place another facial tissue on top of the flowers. Now, carefully turn over another ten pages and place a facial tissue on that page. Proceed as before until you have filled the book. Then place three strong rubber bands around the book to hold it tightly closed. Place a 3-by-5-inch card under the rubber bands with the date, name, and color of the flowers. Place several books or a coffee can filled with sand on the book to weight it down.

The next day, remove all the facial tissues from the book and replace the flowers in the book to continue pressing. By this rapid removal of moisture away from the flowers, you will remove the problem of water stain, which is the main cause of failure in pressing flowers.

Using a clothespin, pin the tissues to a drying line in the attic and then reuse them another day. Replace the rubber bands around the book to hold it firmly closed and place the data label under the rubber bands. Replace the weight on the book.

The length of time required to press flowers by this method varies from one to three weeks. If you are in no hurry to use them in a project, leave them undisturbed for two weeks. Then open the book carefully and check your treasures. If they are flat and crisp, rather stiff when you pick them up, they are quite dry. Some people recommend removing the flowers to boxes for storage. I prefer leaving them in the book where they can be stored flat and where there is less

To support a large leaf, such as this magnolia, run the stem wire halfway up the back of the leaf and glue it in place with a few dots of thick white craft glue.

chance of damage. Because we have such high humidity where I live (in New Jersey), I then place the entire book (with the label clearly visible) into a plastic bag and seal it. This prevents moisture from seeping back into the pages of the book and subsequently into the dried materials.

This procedure, which I use to press wildflowers, such as buttercups, violets, honeysuckle, nightshade, fern, and Queen Anne's lace, is the same procedure to use for pressing your garden flowers. As you can well imagine, flat-type flowers are the simplest to press. Pansies, geranium florets, and the florets of the hydrangea are good examples. Flowers having thick centers require a different treatment. Before placing them in the book for pressing, place them between two thicknesses of waxed paper and then gently flatten them by stepping on them with the heel of your shoe. Once you have flattened the flower, remove it from the waxed paper before placing it between sheets of facial tissue to continue pressing and drying. Place a heavy weight on the book, such as a coffee can full of sand or pebbles.

Sunlight and fluorescent lighting are enemies of dried flowers, so it is important that you protect your flowers from these unusually strong sources of light. Flower prints I made in 1961 have been hanging on the wall in my daughter's room for many years, exposed to incandescent lighting and normal daylight. Their colors are still vivid and lovely.

Press an assortment of individual flower petals too, as they will be helpful when you begin to use your pressed collection in projects. Rose petals are heart-shaped. Bright yellow and orange marigold petals and blue bachelor button, delphinium, and larkspur petals are especially attractive as fillers in a pressed design.

The second method is a speedy way to press a great many flowers. It requires the use of a microwave oven and silica gel. It also requires the use of a pressing book for thirty minutes to preflatten the flowers.

Pick the flowers to be pressed and place them on facial tissues in a pressing book. Use rubber bands to hold the book closed and weight down the book to help press the flowers flat. Preheat a container of silica gel to make sure it is quite dry. (The crystals will be bright blue throughout the desiccant.) Then place a 1-inch-deep bed of silica gel in the bottom of a casserole. Carefully open the pressing book and remove the flowers that have been flattening there for half an hour. Place them on the silica gel in the casserole. Now cover the flowers with an inch of silica gel or more to add weight to the flowers as they press dry.

Using this method, you will have beautifully pressed, brightly colored flowers to work with in just twelve to twenty-four hours instead of two to three weeks!

The fastest way possible to press flowers is the third method. It also requires the use of a microwave oven and, through the magic of microwaves, will give you lovely, perfectly pressed flowers to use within *minutes*!

Follow the directions for the second method up to the part where you have placed the flowers on the silica gel in the casserole. Then cover the flowers with just one inch of preheated silica gel to cover them and hold them flat. Place the casserole in your microwave oven on "high," for just one minute. Then remove the casserole from the microwave oven and set it aside for thirty minutes. At this point, the flowers should be ready for immediate use in a pressed flower project.

CAPTURING FLOWER SCENTS

Every time I dry a lovely flower, I secretly wish I could also preserve its heavenly scent. Although we cannot preserve a flower scent in fact, there are ways of capturing the perfume of the garden.

Potpourri Sachets

For spring and summer dried arrangements, I like to add a potpourri mainly of roses and lavender. The procedure is simple and gratifying.

To help you gauge quantities, it will help you to know that two quarts of fresh rose petals will equal only one quart of dried petals.

To begin, remove and discard the bitter white or green ends from the rose petals. Spread two quarts of rose petals on a screen, in a dry, warm, well-ventilated dark room, such as an attic, to thoroughly dry. If you have lavender growing in your garden, spread one quart of flowers on a screen to dry. If you do not have an attic, a warm furnace room or water heater closet will do. If you have not grown lavender in your garden this year, you may be able to purchase some from a roadside stand or a hobby store that handles the dried lavender. In this case, the lavender will already be dried so you will not have to dry it further.

When the rose petals and lavender are quite dry, place them in a bowl and stir to mix well. Add one tablespoon of orris root powder, as a fixative. This is obtainable at a pharmacy. Again, stir well. Add one tablespoon of grated lemon rind and stir again. Next, add a tablespoon of dried, crushed mint leaves and stir the mixture carefully.

Place this wonderful concoction into a jar with a tight seal. A screw-on lid with a good gasket is ideal. Date the jar. Shake or stir the mixture occasionally, and, in six weeks, your potpourri will be ready to use in tiny sachet bags. Make the sachet bags of nylon net or cheesecloth and, when filled, tuck them into your dried arrangements, bureau drawers, and linen closets. Save some for the umbrella stand by the front door.

If you are satisfied with the scent, you may wish to make more to give as gifts. Because fragrance is a matter of individual preference, experiment until you come up with the perfect combination for your taste. If you would like the aroma to be more lemony, add more grated lemon rind or dried, crushed lemon balm leaves. If you would like the scent a bit spicier, add one tablespoon of powdered cinnamon, allspice, or nutmeg. Also a tablespoon of ground ginger is nice when added to the rose and lavender potpourri.

For sachets to add to autumn dried arrangements, I like dried carnation petals for their spicy aroma.

The Japanese have a quaint custom of placing their favorite herbs underneath the welcome mat at the front door. As callers step on the mat, the crushed herbs release their aroma. A similarly delightful welcome can greet your guests if you sprinkle your potpourri mixture under the welcome mat. This greeting would be especially nice if you were giving a bridal or baby shower.

Floral Concentrates

Another way of capturing the delicate floral scents of the garden for later enjoyment is to make a concentrate. This is easy to do. Start by collecting two quarts of rose petals and removing the bitter green or white ends from each petal. Then, in a bean pot with a tight-fitting lid or other crockery-type vessel, layer rose petals, alternating with coarse salt. Add layers of lavender, alternating with the salt and layers of carnation petals and salt.

Repeat the layers, using mostly fragrant rose petals, until the container is full. Cover tightly and let the crock remain undisturbed in a cool basement for six weeks to purify. At the end of six weeks, strain the contents of the crock through filter paper. Bottle the liquid recovered and cork tightly.

One drop of this essence will perfume a *pint* of water. This delicately scented water is luxuriant to use in your bath, to rinse your hair with, and to rinse lingerie, scarves, and hosiery, and, if dabbed on a *cool* light bulb, when the bulb becomes hot, it will fill the room with a lovely fragrance. Needless to say, it is lovely for gift giving.

ARRANGING FLOWERS PAINLESSLY

When you look at some of the color photographs of arrangements in this book, if you have never made an arrangement before, you may feel overwhelmed. As with anything else, one step at a time is the best advice. Before you know it, you will have completely amazed yourself by finishing your first design. As you sit back to survey your handiwork, you will be filled with enthusiasm and anxious to begin your next arrangement. Something else will happen too. You will know instinctively what you like best about this first arrangement and what you will wish to delete from the second one. Perhaps the arrangement will prove to be larger than you had planned (or smaller) and perhaps you would like to make it again using different colors. At any rate, your first try at flower arranging will be a learning experience, as will every arrangement you ever make. This art form is challenging, stimulating, and always rewarding.

To begin, decide where your arrangement will be used so you

This sketch shows a well-rounded circular arrangement of flowers – one that can be enjoyed from all sides. This is the most common type of arrangement to use for centerpieces.

Oval arrangements are similar to circular ones in that they are pleasing to view from all angles. An oval design, being taller, is not as appropriate for a centerpiece as a circular one.

Triangular arrangements are easy to create and are generally one sided. They are often, therefore, displayed where it is not necessary or desirable to see the back, such as on a foyer table or mantel.

can choose an appropriate container. Cut a piece of floral foam to fit the container, extending 2 inches above the rim. Glue the foam into the container. To conceal the foam, pin tufts of sheet moss all over it with stem wire hairpins. Select the flowers and foliage you wish to use and stem those that require it. Decide on the best filler for your design and the shape.

It will soon become apparent to you that each arrangement consists of four main elements: the line-establishing materials, the filler, the focal point, and the flowers to be displayed.

The line materials are those leaves, branches, or filler that give your arrangement the shape that the rest of the design will follow. For instance, if you wish to create an *L*-shaped arrangement, you would first create an *L*-shape which will guide you in creating the rest of the arrangement. You would use the "filler" material to fill out the *L*-shape and create a "bed" on which to build your arrangement. The focal point of an arrangement is the most important part of the design. It is usually your prettiest or most perfect bloom and the flower you wish the viewer to notice first. Sometimes there is but one focal point. At other times you may have three or more similar flowers that are excitingly special, and these will become the focal points of an arrangement in which they are featured.

In the following illustrations I have given the five most commonly used line arrangements and the three most popular mass arrangements. (See figures.) The circular, oval, and triangular type arrangements are called "mass arrangements." The crescent, vertical, horizontal, right angle, and Hogarth curve shapes, in floral design, are called "line arrangements," and are usually quite dramatic, making a strong statement wherever they are placed. Notice the types of containers used to create each design. The choice of container has a great deal to do with the success of your overall design and actually becomes a part of it.

For your first try at making a dried arrangement, use the most common shape, one that can be viewed pleasingly from any angle. As you progress with your flower preservation skills, you will want to try each of the forms of floral design, and, as you become more expert in arranging the flowers and other dried, natural materials, you will want to pay special attention to the colors you are combining, to the texture of the petals and foliage, and you will constantly check for good balance. It will not take you long to discover which flower colors look nicest together and that by separating colored flowers with white ones or with appropriate foliage, an ordinary arrangement can become quite special. (By separating the colored flowers with white, the individual colors stand out rather than blend into each other.) The heavy, textured petals found on zinnias make a sturdy-looking arrangement. For this reason they look best in a large basket or bold type of container. The more delicate flowers, such as roses, delphiniums, ageratum, and feverfew, look best in a porcelain or lightweight container. As far as balance is concerned, it is simply a matter of standing back from your arrangement during construction to see whether one side of the arrangement is becoming heavy with flowers while the other side of the design is being neglected. Also, the heavier-looking part of the arrangement should be the bottom where the larger flowers are used. To place the flowers otherwise would give you a "top-heavy" design.

For your first arrangement decide where you would like to have flowers enhance a room. Determine if you would like the flowers to contrast with the color scheme of the room or to blend with it. Decide how much space can be devoted to the arrangement without having the flowers overpower the room. On the other hand, you do not want to make a design that will be so small that it will go unnoticed. You definitely want your design to become an integral part of the decoration of the room in which it is placed.

If you have a family room or den, for instance, with dark-paneled walls, you can add brightness by creating a warm, vibrant arrangement of sunny colors. To make an arrangement in dark, woody colors would be to make an arrangement that would vanish right into the walls. Fortunately, the hues of most flowers blend nicely together, making it easy to plan a harmonious color scheme.

After you have settled on the colors you will use, decide the shape of your design. Again, I usually recommend that the first arrangement be a small, round centerpiece in a container about the size of a half grapefruit. Circular or oval-shaped arrangements are easy to put together using German statice, baby's breath, or gypsy broom to help round out the shape. An arrangement of this shape can be used on a dining table, end table, coffee table, bookshelves, powder room vanity, or bedside table. It also makes a lovely gift and is easy to wrap and transport.

Triangular, one-sided arrangements are also easy to achieve, and you will find several examples of this shape among the color photographs in this book. They are used in places where it is not necessary to have the back on display, such as against a wall, in the foyer, on a buffet, under a painting in a hallway, on a mantel, or on a corner table.

Now, finally, think scale—the relationship between parts of a design: the size of the flowers, their placement for good balance, and how the entire arrangement looks in proportion to the container.

The container should relate well to the flowers in color and height. A general rule of thumb to help you obtain good balance is for the design to be two and a half times the height of the vase. This is a broad gauge that usually works well. Experiment. You may prefer to make an arrangement a little taller or a little shorter, depending on where it will be used when finished. The taller the arrangement, the more airy and lightweight the floral material should be toward the top and outer edges or it will look top-heavy.

If you have determined your color scheme, the shape of the design you are going to make, and realize the importance of checking for scale periodically, you are ready to begin your first arrangement.

Relax! It's going to be fun. Don't try to complete it in thirty

The crescent-shaped floral design would form a circle if the lines were extended. If you keep this in mind while working on your arrangement, it will guide you in forming a good crescent design.

The L or right-angle arrangement is suitable for use in any corner or asymmetrical position in most any room of the house. It is especially attractive in contemporary settings.

Horizontal arrangements are often used for dining table centerpieces because they are low enough to see over.

Named for the English artist, William Hogarth, the Hogarth curve is one of the most interesting and difficult lines in flower arrangement. Basically, it consists of two half circles that join at or near the focal point and flow in opposite directions from that point to form a standard or reverse S.

minutes. Enjoy working with the materials and seeing the design emerge. Work a while, take a break, and walk away from it. Then go back to it, refreshed, and begin again.

To make a small, round centerpiece, you can use a 5-inch-diameter basket, a silver or pewter bowl, or a china or wooden bowl, depending on where the arrangement will ultimately be used and the flower colors you have chosen for the design. Cut a 3- to 4-inch square of floral foam. Round the top, sides, and bottom to fit the container by trimming with a small knife. This foam base should extend an inch above the rim of the container. Apply rubber cement to the bottom of the foam if you are going to use a glass or china-type container, and glue it in place. If you are using a basket, hot glue or heavy white glue will work best. For a metal or wooden bowl, you may wish to use green floral tape made especially for anchoring foam into containers. The tape goes over the foam in several directions and sticks to the container, just below the outside rim. The base of the arrangement must have stability. If it wobbles, use more glue or tape, or wait for the glue to dry.

Because the mechanics of an arrangement are not attractive and can actually detract from an otherwise pretty design, it is important to conceal them. Pin sheet moss all over floral foam. Make the pins from small pieces of stem wire formed in the shape of a hairpin. Do not glue moss on the foam or you will be unable to penetrate the foam with the flower stems once the glue has dried. Some designers recommend covering the foam base with small pieces of German statice, gypsy broom, or broom bloom. Since these fillers are expensive, I prefer to use them in the arrangement where they will be seen. Sheet moss can be purchased cheaply, stretched to cover many pieces of foam, or even gathered and dried yourself.

Once you have chosen your container and prepared your foam base, you are ready to begin the actual design.

In dried arrangements a filler material is used to outline the basic shape of the arrangement. The most common fillers are German statice, baby's breath, and gypsy broom. The easiest of these to work with is the gypsy broom because the stems are usually quite straight. You can place a straight stem exactly where you wish it to go in creating your basic shape. German statice is an excellent filler, but, because of its curvy nature, it takes a little getting used to. It adds showy white, graceful lines to any arrangement. Baby's breath is a delicate, white filler. It is easier to use small pieces of baby's breath to round out a finished arrangement than it is to create the shape of the design with it. Bristol fairy is one of the best varieties of baby's breath because it has larger blossoms than most. The illustration shows clearly how to place the filler in a "step-down" fashion, from tallest flowers to medium height, to the very low ones at the base and around the edge of the container. (See figure.)

Begin by inserting your filler evenly all around the edge of the container. The idea is to make a little edging around the container, extending about 2 inches out from the container. When you are satisfied with this step, establish the height of your arrangement by inserting the tallest piece of filler in the center of the arrangement. Most often, this tall piece is equal to two and a half times the height of the container or width of the container, whichever is greatest. Once the height is established, work down from that point with other pieces of filler until you have a well-shaped basket or container of filler that looks pleasing to you.

When you are satisfied with the shape of your arranged filler, you will be ready to add a heavier filler in between the gypsy broom for body. You may use goldenrod, feathery celosia, white or blue statice, or glycerinized fern. Add some of this material deep into the bouquet for depth and contrast, and insert some to extend 3 to 4 inches out of the arrangement to add to the shape, as well as for good background material. If these heavier fillers seem too large for good scale, break them into smaller pieces, dip them in glue, and glue them to the gypsy broom.

Vertical arrangements are perfect for either end of a mantel, as they are tall and simple. This line is also excellent for floor-type arrangements.

Your centerpiece should now appear nicely rounded and ready for you to add the main flowers. This is the time to add tall spike-type material, such as blue sage, delphinium or larkspur, bridal wreath, heather, wild oats, or barley. Place the most feathery, lightest piece, at the top center, extending 2 inches higher than the filler. Continue inserting your choice of spike-type material, using about eleven total, equally distributed throughout the arrangement. (See figure.)

Helichrysum, the common strawflower, is sturdy and easy to work with for your first arrangement. This is the time to add it to your arrangement. Place the smallest flower at top center. Insert three medium-sized ones next, about halfway down the arrangement, forming a triangle below the top flower. Insert five of your largest helichrysums next around the rim of your container, extending 2 to 3 inches over the rim, in an irregular line around the arrangement.

Make sure the flowers do not touch each other and that they are separated by space and filler. Some of your flowers may be glued directly to the filler material, some flowers will have stems that can be inserted into the moss-covered base, and others may require stemming with floral tape and wire. (See figures on pages 30 and 31.)

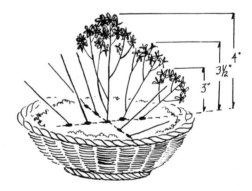

To create a well-rounded base of filler material it is necessary to insert the filler stems at an angle, as shown in this sketch.

At this point, your creation should look magnificent! If one piece seems to stand out of line with the others, use your pliers to grasp the stem and push it into the foam a little deeper. Should the largest flowers at the rim of the container seem to be standing out too far from the rest of the design, try inserting their stems deeper into the foam or glue bunches of baby's breath in between the large flower heads and the filler. In the case of the latter, it will then be necessary to glue more bunches of baby's breath throughout the arrangement to tie it all together.

If selecting your flowers, stemming them, spraying them with a sealer to prevent them from reabsorbing moisture from the air, and readying your container with the foam base before actually constructing your arrangement seem a bit tedious to you, perhaps you will enjoy working in this medium more if you divide the project over several days. One day you can select and prepare several containers.

Another day you can select flowers that will go well with the containers you will be using and will complement the decor of the room in which the arrangements will be placed. Once selected, you will want to spray and stem the flowers. Using a brick of Sahara or Ultra-foam, insert the newly stemmed flowers in an upright position where they will be easily accessible as you work with them. Perhaps the next day you will be able to begin your first arrangement, with all your thoughts centering on the composition of that design.

Now that the mysteries of flower arranging have all dissolved, and you have become an overnight success at it, why not choose one of the designs pictured in this book for your next project? Select one that will fit well into your decorative scheme. Decide where it will be placed when finished, choose the colors and container best for that room, and, *voilà*, you're on your way!

USES OF PARAFFIN

Paraffin is a most important part of my flower preservation technique. I keep a box of household paraffin wax, the type used for sealing homemade jams and jellies, in my supply cabinet. Old candles may be added to the wax-melting container, and the wicks removed later.

To use paraffin, it must be melted until it reaches the point resembling clear water. To do this I place the wax in a coffee can, then place the can in a pan of hot water on the range. As the water reaches boiling, the wax will rapidly begin to melt. Because the temperature of the water will not go above 212°F., neither will the temperature of the wax. *Never melt wax unless the container is seated in a pan of water.* In this way you can control the temperature of the wax and thus avoid overheating it by accident. Wax is flammable if *overheated* or exposed to an open flame or heated in an oven, so *never melt directly* in a pan over fire, hotplate, sterno, or on a kitchen range. Check often to make sure the water has not evaporated from the pan.

When the wax has become quite watery in appearance, remove it from the range and place the container on a breadboard. Be sure to cover your work area with newspaper.

The following are some of the many ways in which I use paraffin.

Berries: Blue juniper and viburnum berries, fiery orange pyracantha, and bittersweet berries, lavender-pink beauty berries, and rosy pepper berries are among my favorite berries for drying. If you dip small branches of these berries into melted wax, two good things will happen. The wax will seal the berries onto the stem making them longer lasting and enabling you to use them on door wreaths or other arrangements where frequent jostlings would otherwise cause them to drop off. The wax will also seal indentations on the berries caused by dehydration as they were drying, and make them appear more plump. If the wax has been melted to the watery consistency, it will dry clear on the berries. If you have used the wax while some of it was still milky, the berries will have a whitish cast. This can be effective in a winter arrangement where white is preferred. To avoid flat spots, drain well, and hold the cluster in your hand until it is quite dry and stiff.

Flowers: Some flowers, such as azalea, rhododendron, day lily, catalpa blooms, crocus, dogwood, and pansies (to name just a few), last longer in humid areas if they are back-coated with paraffin. For this procedure, I use a small artist's brush reserved for this purpose. Paint the stemmed blossom with melted wax from the stem right up over the calyx (where the petals are connected to the stem) and out to the tips of the petal. I hold the flower upside down while the wax dries thoroughly. The wax then supports the total flower. If humidity should reach these blossoms, they will not wilt because the wax is supporting them.

I also reinforce roses that are rather full-blown, even though I have already dropped Duco cement inside of the blooms prior to drying them. By coating the back of the roses with wax, their petal structure is strengthened.

Domes and jars: Dried arrangements are frequently sealed under glass or Lucite domes or in glass decorative jars. If the flowers are first reinforced with wax, they will be stronger and better able to take the bumping around they may receive while being dusted and polished. Also, if you seal the dome or jar with melted paraffin, it will be easier to open in the event you wish to redo the arrangement or make an entirely different one in the same container. By holding an ice cube to the wax seal, it will crack, enabling you to open the container with ease. To camouflage a wax seal glue moss-green velvet baby's ribbon trim around the outside of the dome or jar base.

Mushrooms: Because mushrooms are mostly water, their caps shrivel while drying. To fill in the crevices and to make the caps smoother, dip them in melted paraffin. If the wax is clear and watery, the color and natural appearance will not be changed.

Candles: To add a special charm to a dried arrangement, I frequently make a floating candle and anchor it in the front of the arrangement to stabilize it. My arrangement, Summer Memories (page 81), is a good example of this. Sometimes, I use a hummingbird cup (gourd), and fill it with melted paraffin (first lining the cup with foil) to make a "natural container" candle to go with an arrangement.

The floating candle is simple to make, yet it adds an exotic finish to a design that is long lasting. Using a seashell or any preferred mold, oil it and chill before using. Then melt the wax to a watery consistency and pour it into the mold. As the wax begins to harden, it will become slightly milky in appearance. This takes about five to ten minutes. At this point, insert a piece of wire-core wick (available at craft stores). This type of wick will stand up in the congealing wax without the necessity of a weight to hold it in place. When the candle is cool and thoroughly hardened, it will have a depression around the wick. Melt more paraffin and fill in the depression to make the top level.

If you wish to make a container candle in a gourd or votive candle holder, you need not oil the mold. Simply melt the wax as before, until clear and watery; then pour it into the container to the desired level. When the wax begins to set and becomes milky, insert the wire-core wick. As with the floating candle, there will be a depression at the center of the candle to fill once the wax hardens. Heat the wax and fill in the center for a long-burning, cheery candle.

The floating candle in my Summer Memories arrangement is anchored to three white pebbles which are attached to the black container with floral clay.

Paraffin may also be used as a substitute for floral clay. It will anchor needlepoint holders in place, and can be used to hold statues, rocks, and shells in a design similar to Summer Memories. In short, it's indispensable.

FOUR SEASONS OF PROJECTS

George Santayana once made the observation: "To be interested in the changing seasons is a happier state of mind than to be hopelessly in love with spring."

In the next four sections of the book, I have tried to provide you with an orderly game plan of seasonal projects and activities, starting with spring . . . the season of growth and renewal. If you are a beginner, the logical sequence of the remaining seasonal activities will ease you into this fascinating art. The well-seasoned enthusiasts among you will enjoy reviewing some ideas you may have forgotten.

SPRING

With the arrival of spring, the miracle season is with us once again. The gentle rains come, the warm sun shines, and our world turns green again. The gray trees, beige lawns, and sleeping gardens come alive, and so do we. Tiny blossoms of every pastel shade cover the fruit trees and shrubs.

The crocus is the first to poke its head through the melting snow in my garden. The children are so excited as they announce its arrival! From that moment on, the winter doldrums flee and our spirits are high as we begin plans for our spring and summer activities.

High on my list of priorities is the garden, and, as you may have discovered, a beautiful flower garden doesn't just happen. It takes very careful planning, forethought, and lots of time and work.

To plant a garden larger than can be properly cared for would be to take all the pleasure from it. The chores of weeding, watering, and fertilizing can become overwhelming in the heat of the summer. So, as much as you would like to plant one of everything pictured in the seed catalogs, try to contain yourself. Keep in mind that this year you will be drying and preserving flowers, as well as tending them in the garden (and, since we are becoming more water-conservation conscious than ever, it is especially important not to plant more than you can easily care for).

If the seeds you ordered have arrived, it is time to carefully coordinate the blooming times, flower color combinations, and heights the flowers will reach.

For a constant display of colors complementary to each other in spectrum and scale, you will want to plant some of each type of seed two weeks apart. Check the seed packets for expected heights of the plants, so that you do not, in your enthusiasm, plant some 6-footers where the border plants should be.

A good practice that eventually leads to effortless gardening is to purchase at least one good perennial every spring. One such flower that dries well and returns perennially to your garden is the peony, which now comes in every imaginable color except blue. It requires lots of sun but is not particular about the type of soil you plant it in, as long as it is well drained. (Refer to the Quick Reference Chart for drying information.) Peony leaves are beautiful in arrangements when preserved in glycerin or when pressed.

Candytuft dries beautifully and adds that all-important white to arrangements. Although it is very short stemmed, growing mostly in rock gardens or as an edging, its blooms dry to perfection in silica gel and can be stemmed or glued into an arrangement.

Blue salvia is a perennial in mild climates, blooms all summer and fall, and air dries beautifully. The salvia species, *Farinacea victoria*, produces dense flowered spikes of intense violet-blue and is my favorite.

The Iceland poppy is a long-stemmed perennial that comes in many brilliant shades of red, pink, orange, and yellow. It will produce blooms the first year if sown early. In the South and Pacific Southwest, sow the seeds in the early fall, for the following spring. The Champagne Bubbles Hybrid Iceland poppy has stronger stems than most varieties of Iceland poppy and a long blooming period.

The oriental poppy is also a perennial, blooming profusely in May and June with very showy, large, brilliantly colored blooms.

The *Scabiosa caucasica* is a perennial, producing long-stemmed flowers 2 to 3 inches across, in azure to deep blue, pale lavender, and white. They bloom from early summer to fall.

The columbine has a graceful, airy, complicated-looking blossom that dries to perfection in silica gel. Being a perennial, it will thrill you with flowers to dry, year after year. It prefers a fairly rich, well-drained soil, in either full sun or semi-shade.

These are just a few of the dryable flowers that will appear, as if by magic, in your garden every year with dependable regularity, giving you more time to devote to the annuals planted each spring for drying.

You may already have some of these old reliables in your garden, and perhaps you never dreamed you could preserve them. If you have any of the following, you have a head start in drying a collection of beautiful flowers.

Ageratum	Dutch hyacinth
Ajuga	Grape hyacinth
Azaleas	Hydrangea
Bridal wreath	Lilac
Crocus (more than seventy-five species)	Mock orange
	Pussy willow
Daffodil (innumerable varieties)	Rhododendron
Dogwood	Roses

Silk and Dried Flowers Wedding Bouquet

It has always seemed a pity to me that the lovely wedding flowers chosen to highlight the beauty and happiness of the most special day in one's life barely make it through the reception.

The major objection I have heard regarding the use of silk and dried flowers for a wedding is that there is no scent. This objection may be overcome by simply saturating a piece of cotton with the bride's favorite perfume and tucking it among the filler of the bouquets. I also add a glass vial containing water to the bouquets and then insert three fresh roses or daisies or a gardenia in the vial just before the wedding. When the flowers wilt, the vial is removed and the filler fluffed over the small space. So, you can see it *is* possible to have all three, the silk and dried bouquets, the fresh flowers, and the lovely floral scent!

I made the illustrated bridal bouquet for my daughter Sherri's wedding to Dave. The maid of honor's bouquet, made for my daughter, Debbie, had a beautiful rose center; the tiny bouquet is called a "throwaway" bouquet. (When making a lovely keepsake bridal bouquet, you certainly do not want the bride tossing it, so a small, throwaway bouquet is always used for that purpose.)

Wedding memories . . . a bridal keepsake. How nice to have them preserved in this lovely silk and dried flower bouquet to be cherished for years to come.

Materials

1 nosegay bouquet holder, 8-inch diameter, with floral foam
large, empty, glass soda bottle (or clay flowerpot)
German statice
spring green gypsy broom
8 silk dieffenbachia leaves, 5-inch long
8 short wooden floral picks
14 shell pink silk rosebuds
17 white net puffs on picks
6 medium-size white silk roses
3 white silk vanda orchids
2 bunches lily of the valley
2 bunches stephanotis
6 yards ½-inch-wide velvet ribbon, white
thick white craft glue
wire, 24-gauge
wire cutters
scissors
green floral tape

The maid-of-honor's bouquet contains some of the same flowers used in the bridal bouquet and features a lovely pink rose in the center – to match the color of her gown. Maidenhair fern outlines the nosegay design.

Instructions

1. Insert the handle of the bouquet holder into the soda bottle or inverted flowerpot to hold it while you work.

2. Cover the foam in your bouquet holder with short pieces of German statice.

3. In between the statice, add small pieces of spring green gypsy

This tiny "throwaway" bouquet is tossed in place of the bridal bouquet.

To make a net puff simply gather a 3- or 4-inch square of nylon net at the raw ends and wire it to a floral pick. Net puffs are good fillers in wedding and prom bouquets and add a soft, feminine touch.

An unusual wedding bouquet, designed to look as though the bride had just picked the roses from her garden.

A hat with a garland to match the bride's bouquet.

broom, allowing them to extend out from the statice about an inch.

4. Cut silk dieffenbachia leaves from their stem and wire each leaf onto a wooden floral pick.

5. Insert one leaf at the top of the bouquet holder and one at the bottom. Next add the remaining leaves around the outside edges of the bouquet, three to each side. The top and bottom leaves should extend a little farther out than the side leaves in order to start your elongated shape.

6. Next, remove all leaves from the pink silk rosebuds and set them aside for use later.

7. Insert one pink rosebud into the bouquet foam, at a slight angle (facing up and out) directly over each dieffenbachia leaf. The one at the top and the one at the bottom should extend a little farther out than the side ones for shape.

8. Add longer pieces of German statice beside each pink rose (4-inch lengths are good).

9. Next, add a net puff above each rose at an angle. Do not allow the net to touch the rose. (See figure.)

10. Add the six white medium roses and six more of the pink rosebuds, alternating them in a circle above the first row of roses.

11. Circle the flowers inserted in step 10 with net puffs above each pink rose.

12. Add longer stems of German statice to raise the crown of your bouquet and add the white orchids on top of the "crown" filler.

13. Cut each lily of the valley stem and stephanotis stem from their bunches.

14. Stem and tape each of the above flowers. A 6-inch stem should be sufficient.

15. Insert lily of the valley stems in between each dieffenbachia leaf and encircle the top layer of orchids with them.

16. Add the stephanotis blossoms in an irregular pattern for realism, allowing them to extend out beyond the bouquet slightly.

17. Apply glue to the silk rose leaves, and insert them around the upper circle of pink and white roses.

18. Using the ribbon, add streamers to the handle with hot glue or thick white craft glue.

Wedding bouquets come in many styles, shapes, and sizes. Sherri's was a modified cascade because Sherri is tiny. A larger bride might like to have a bouquet with a longer cascade. It is important that the bouquet not look as though it is taking the bride down the aisle, and that, most importantly, it reflect the style and taste of the bride. Because Sherri enjoys houseplants, I used the dieffenbachia leaves to outline her modified cascade bouquet.

Lori Del Gesso wanted her bouquet to be entirely of white roses and to look as though she had just picked them from the garden. The result is sketched for you to see. Each rose was given a long stem, the stems were then fastened together with floral tape and hot glue, silk fern and rose leaves were added to separate the roses so they would not blend into each other, and bridal lace streamers were attached to the stem end of the bouquet, which complemented the lace in Lori's gown. I also decorated Lori's beautiful picture hat, creating a garland of the same type white silk roses.

Scrub Brush Spring Garden

This precious mini-garden adds just the right topping to a basket of cleaning supplies, kitchen utensils, and other useful gifts for the bride-to-be or for a housewarming.

It is made on a natural bristle scrub brush banded in moss-green velvet ribbon. The little gardener was actually a Christmas tree ornament. The ribbon and doll are glued to the bristles.

The background "tall trees" are pieces of sea beach dock, but any tall dried material will suffice. It is glued to the bristles with thick white craft glue, which will dry clear and will peel off the bristles when the brush eventually is used.

Tiny pieces of German statice, yarrow, tansy, a pine cone, and some rhododendron pods complete this garden. However, any assortment of tiny dried flowers may be used.

Whenever I make an arrangement, I save the leftover tiny pieces of flowers in a special box. They are perfect for projects such as this decorated scrub brush. Another use for the leftovers, as shown here, is in decorating place cards for a party, notepaper, and package tags.

Still another use for these tiny scraps is in making *bobeches* (candlestick collars that catch wax as it drips). Trace a 3-inch circle onto plastic cut from a milk carton. Cut out the circle and a ⅞-inch inner circle. Using thick white craft glue, cover the plastic circle with green moss to make a mini-wreath. Glue flowers from your scrap box to decorate the wreath. When completed the little wreaths are used on candlesticks as decorations and to catch any wax that might drip from a taper. Sets of these mini-wreaths make lovely yet inexpensive gifts. If done all in white flowers they make nice wedding gifts. When Christmas colored flowers and hemlock cones are used, they take on a holiday flavor and, for fall entertaining, I use the golds, browns, and oranges of autumn.

Country Mouse Spring Bouquet

This little arrangement shows the importance of "playing down" when using a novelty-type container such as this one. A light, airy arrangement does not detract from the design of the container, but rather enhances it. It is important that the floral design and container do not vie for attention.

Materials

    container in an appropriate shape
    floral foam
    moss
    assortment of lightweight, feathery, ornamental grasses and delicate berries, such as beauty berries, jet bead, viburnum

A scrub brush is the last place you would expect to find a garden and a perky little gardener! Fast and simple to make, it will delight any bride-to-be or gardener.

This pretty place card is fast and easy to make from leftover flowers or pressed blooms. It makes a nice momento of a special occasion.

Your pattern for a bobeche *candle wreath, with which you can decorate a brass or pewter candlestick, should look like this.*

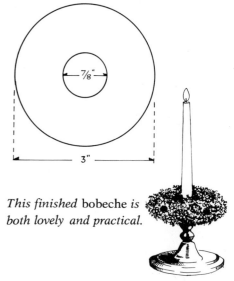

This finished bobeche *is both lovely and practical.*

white statice and German statice

assortment of heather, goldenrod, blue sage, gypsy broom, and pepper-grass in colors that harmonize with the colors in the container

stem wire

wire cutters

thick white craft glue

scissors

Instructions

1. Cut a piece of floral foam to fit the opening of your container and to extend 2 inches above the edge of the opening.

2. Glue and wedge it firmly in place.

3. Cover floral foam with moss pinned on with stem wire pins (see page 37 for directions).

4. Add the tallest, most feathery material first, creating the height and width you wish the arrangement to be.

5. Insert pieces of German statice next, about 5 to 6 inches in length, to give depth to the design.

6. Finish off the background for this type of container by adding any of the listed types of material which would pick up a color on the container or accent the general color theme of the container.

You have not made what we normally think of as an arrangement, but rather you have created a pleasing background against which you may display this particular type of container.

Notice that I have brought some pieces of the material around the sides of the skirt on the left and over the shoulder, on the right, to bring the country mouse *into* the arrangement. I also glued a tiny bouquet in her hands.

This can be an easy-to-make gift for a child who is confined to the house or hospital, especially if you use one of their favorite storybook or television character containers.

Decorative Hanging Sphere

I find this hanging sphere a refreshing departure from the hanging planter. You will enjoy making this project, as it goes together quickly and merely involves gluing stemless flowers (helichrysums are best) and hemlock cones or globe amaranths all over the foam ball.

The hot glue gun will allow you to work rapidly, as the glue will set up immediately. Thick white craft glue will also work well, but takes longer for the glue to set. Depending on the size hanging you desire, choose a foam ball for your base. I used a 6-inch styrofoam ball for this design and the finished ball was 8 inches in diameter.

Materials

one 6-inch styrofoam ball

1 hanging chain (a bamboo or wicker-link one is especially nice)

1 soup bowl

This country-mouse background design can be done in any novelty-type container. A child would appreciate a favorite TV or storybook character container. The design technique would be the same.

assortment of helichrysums (common strawflower) (the number varies with the size of the flowers)

tufts of red celosia

assortment of hemlock cones or globe amaranths

2 yards gingham ribbon, green

purple, pink, yellow, white, or blue statice

hot glue and glue gun, or thick white craft glue

6 inches strong wire for hanger

wire cutters

scissors

Instructions

1. Glue a strong piece of wire into the top of the styrofoam ball and attach the hanging chain. The ball should hang just a little above eye level. Place the ball in a soup bowl to hold it steady while you are working on it.

2. Begin gluing flowers on the ball, starting at the top and keeping the flower heads very close together. You do not want to leave any space between flowers larger than can be covered with a hemlock cone or globe amaranth.

3. When you have covered the ball two-thirds of the way, go over it and fill in any space with tiny hemlock cones or globe amaranths.

4. At this point, if you are using white craft glue, let your project set overnight. If you are using the hot glue gun, hang the ball on a wall hook or handle of a cupboard door in order to finish applying the flowers to the bottom of the ball.

5. Attach a pretty gingham bow with streamers to the bottom of the ball with hot glue, or, if you are using white craft glue, wrap a short stem of wire around the center of your bow, coat the wire with glue, and insert it into the ball.

This method of creating a floral ball can also be used for making a kissing ball for a Christmas decoration. For the kissing ball, use a 4-inch styrofoam ball and glue small pine cones, sweet gum balls, and fresh boxwood leaves all over it. Attach mistletoe with red velvet ribbon streamers at the bottom of the ball. Use red velvet ribbon to hang the ball.

Contemporary Arrangement

When a friend called to ask me if I could make an arrangement to be given to the owner of a newly opened beauty salon, and told me the color scheme was burgundy, silver, black, gray, and white, an interesting design resulted. Nothing like starting the day off with a real challenge!

Because the arrangement was needed to decorate a large salon, size was a major consideration. In order to create a container of appropriate size, I glued two square silver planters together with hot glue. Each side of my double container was then fitted with moss-covered floral foam, extending 2 inches above the rim. A 3-inch square of floral foam was glued to the container where the planters were joined.

In recent years, hanging baskets have become popular. This decorative hanging sphere can take the place of a hanging basket and add an original touch wherever it is hung. It can be made of an assortment of flowers or all one type, such as this ball of helichrysums. I have glued hemlock cones between the flowers.

A contemporary challenge! Given an unusual color scheme with which to work . . . the above design of silver, black, red, gray, and white was created to complement the decor of a new beauty salon.

I made an outline of the triangular shape I wanted to construct, with soft, pale green, field-grass stalks. I then outlined the same triangle using gray sage and off-white dactilo. Green and white gypsy broom was used for the filler, and I sprayed ruscus black, to highlight the arrangement and used it as shadow.

I inserted burgundy silk rosebuds on long stems to resemble fresh roses. To continue the burgundy color throughout the arrangement without using additional roses, I sprayed yarrow with cranberry floral paint. The silver-berried spears are milo (sorghum), which I sprayed with bright silver paint to tie in with the container. White Japanese millet and white brizza grass lightened the design, and shiny black jet bead berries completed the composition.

As you can imagine, this was a difficult color combination to work with — incorporating silver and black into the design was the hard part. However, it was extremely satisfying to see how perfectly the arrangement complemented the decor of the new salon.

Mushroom Basket

Mushrooms are popular not only with gourmets but with decorators and designers as well. There is something woodsy and quaint about them, which allows them to fit into any decorative scheme beautifully.

You may use any type of basket for your mushroom arrangement, but I find a little 6-inch market basket to be the most appropriate.

Materials

What could be more provincial looking than a mini market basket filled with mushrooms and tiny dried flowers? Make lots of them for gifts.

By using a paper core for pine cone baskets you will use fewer cones. Pine cones should extend over the rim of the basket, creating a nice edging.

    one 6- to 8-inch market basket
    assortment of bright green sheet moss and blue reindeer moss
    assortment of dried mushrooms
    tiny starflowers, in pastel colors
    bow, green gingham
    newspaper
    hot glue and glue gun, or thick white craft glue
    stem wire
    wire cutters
    scissors

Instructions

1. Make a core of the newspaper (see figure). Tuck the ends of the paper under the core you are forming, until the core becomes firm.

2. Run both ends of a piece of stem wire up through the bottom of the basket and twist them tightly together over the paper core while holding it in place. The paper should be a little higher at the center of the basket.

3. Conceal the newspaper core by covering it with bright green sheet moss. For added interest, patches of the bluish reindeer moss or other type of moss, gathered and dried, can be used with the sheet moss. The moss should

be higher at the center of the basket, giving the effect of a little hill.

4. Next, glue the largest mushrooms you have dried (according to the instructions on page 40) at the top of your moss-covered hill. As the smaller mushrooms are glued to the moss, going down the hill, they take on a jaunty angle which seems to suit them. If you are using hot glue, you will be able to work rapidly. If you are using white craft glue, you may have to prop the angled mushrooms against a stem wire hairpin temporarily, while the glue dries.

5. Leave plenty of space between the mushrooms so that each one may be seen and appreciated separately.

6. From the base of the stem of each mushroom, glue three to five tiny starflowers to appear as though they are growing out from under the mushroom umbrella.

7. A crisp gingham bow attached to the handle of the basket completes your arrangement with a decidedly country flavor. Use a color that complements the room in which the arrangement will be placed.

Now that you have seen how easily this design goes together, I hope you will make several more for your mushroom-loving friends, lest they wheedle yours away from you.

To dry mushrooms choose ones with large caps and long stems. (Because mushrooms are mostly water, they will shrink greatly while drying.) Heat a small bowl full of silica gel in the microwave oven until the crystals are very blue. Do *not* rinse or wet the mushrooms, but brush them off with facial tissue if they are soiled. Then bury one mushroom in the silica gel, upright, so the cap does not flatten. Next, place the bowl of silica gel with the mushroom in the microwave oven for three minutes on "high," then set it aside to be checked in one-half hour. The mushroom should be dry. If not, let it be for another hour.

When the mushroom is dry, remove it to a paper towel and return the silica gel to the oven to thoroughly dry before dehydrating the next mushroom. Continue in this manner until you have dried enough mushrooms to make a mushroom basket or several.

If you do not have a microwave oven, preheat your silica gel in a conventional oven until it is very dry; dry one mushroom per container and let the containers set overnight, covered with plastic food wrap.

Before gluing the mushrooms into the basket, dip each cap into melted paraffin. See Uses of Paraffin.

Walnut Plank Spring Scene

This multifaceted arrangement speaks of spring. A beautiful butterfly is perched on a *Martynia* pod (devil's claw) and seems to be surveying the situation. Spring is represented by the "green underbrush" popping up among the beige and brown survivors of winter. The blue sage and ageratum, the white bridal wreath, and gypsy broom add delicate spring touches to the golden helichrysums and brown feathery heather. A little bird is checking her nest of three eggs, on the left

The theme "a woodsy scene on a walnut plank" gives you carte blanche to design your own little secret world in the forest. Mine is an announcement of spring's arrival. Yours could be Christmas in the woods, using deer and other animals.

The Madonna statue in a garden of roses, daffodils, pussy willow, and ageratum speaks of spring. The same statue surrounded by woody cones and pods, and flowers of gold, orange, and rust would take on a fall flavor.

The little candle creates enough heat to release the fragrance from the potpourri surrounding it, and the pressed flowers on the bubble bowl seem to regain their scent.

side of the arrangement and bluish reindeer moss borders the woodsy scene.

This type of arrangement is one of my favorites. I often include little pebble paths leading into the woods over a mossy trail, tiny rabbits, squirrels, and mushrooms. Sometimes, a little bridge ornament spanning a mirror lake with flowers blooming around its edges, will add a point of interest.

This arrangement is built on a walnut plank. Any rough, rustic-looking plank could be quite effective. The pretty background fan is a large lichen. Behind the lichen are large, spicy-scented cinnamon sticks, arranged in a ray pattern. Camphor pods may be seen tucked into the arrangement to carry the wooden appearance of the plank into the design.

The yellow, 3-by-3-inch foliating candle in the foreground is *not* glued in place. This allows you to replace it with ease and also to pour off the melted wax as it accumulates around the wick. Once the candle burns down about 2 inches from the top, the flame glows through the candle, softly lighting the entire arrangement.

Madonna Garden Scene

To make an arrangement using a statue of any kind, it is imperative to anchor it firmly with floral clay to the base of the design. The base of this "spring garden" is a natural wood plank, and the statue was attached to it before I covered the plank with moss. Also, five small squares of floral foam were glued to the base around the feet of the statue prior to gluing moss over the rest of the plank.

The trellis, offset behind the statue, adds an outdoor garden flavor to this design. The daffodils, rosebuds, tiny blue periwinkle blossoms, pussy willow, and ageratum bring springtime to the arrangement. Sprays of German statice and white African strawflowers add the color separation needed to make the other flowers so effective. For greenery, rose leaves were dried between paper napkins in the microwave oven. Notice how the rosy hue was preserved. The dark green sprays in the background are made of palm leaves split lengthwise, and the greenery in the foreground is carnation leaves which have been air dried.

Any type of statue could be used in making this garden scene. Children would love to see figurines of kittens, dogs, or birds as the focal point, and I have a figurine of a little boy fishing that would look charming in a similar arrangement.

Potpourri Bubble

This delightful arrangement can be made by anyone who happens to have a bubble bowl (a bubble-shaped bowl) handy and some sweetly scented potpourri sachet mix. It is a fun springtime activity, it can be enjoyed by everyone, and it makes a well-received gift for many occasions.

Materials

1 glass bubble bowl, 8-inch diameter (available in dimestores)

1 drinking tumbler of thin glass

floral clay (about the size of a nickle)

votive candle, pink or white

2 packages of potpourri mixture (from a craft store or mail order source) or potpourri mixture you have made

assortment of dry, pressed flowers, leaves, or ferns of your choice

thin, white glue that will dry clear

drinking straw or tongs

Instructions

1. Decorate the bubble bowl by gluing on your dry, pressed flowers, leaves, or ferns.

2. Attach the drinking tumbler to the inside of the bubble bowl, being careful to center it, using a ball of floral clay about the size of a nickel.

3. Pour the dry potpourri mixture into the bowl, surrounding the drinking glass.

4. Add a teaspoonful of water to the inside of the drinking tumbler and then seat a votive candle in the water.

5. Use a drinking straw for lighting the candle and tongs to remove the candle for replacement.

6. As the candle burns, it will heat the side of the glass enough to release the luscious scent of the potpourri permeating the air. When the candle has burned down, the water in the tumbler will extinguish the flame and prevent the glass from cracking.

When not in use, cover your potpourri bubble with plastic food wrap to preserve the aroma, and store it in a closet where it will not be accidentally upset.

By storing this arrangement in your linen closet, any scent that may escape will be quickly captured by the towels and bed linens.

Spring Flowers in an Oriental Basket

This dark brown basket from China is one of exceptional design and excellent craftsmanship. We have started seeing such baskets on the market since trade with China has been resumed. Many of their designs are woven to resemble something other than typical baskets. This one is hexagonal and has a woven lid which fits it perfectly. I have attached the lid to the front of the basket with hot glue in order not to lose part of this exquisite design. (Floral clay could have been used as effectively.)

The focal point of the arrangement is a red peony that I dried five years ago! The pretty green foliage is *Vinca minor* leaves that have been dried in the microwave oven without silica gel.

Most of the filler consists of celery-colored wild sea grass, spring green gypsy broom, and white gypsy. In between these fillers I have inserted stems of coffee grass, a wild reddish-brown grass which

This delicate arrangement in a lovely oriental basket was designed for year-round enjoyment. It is 11 inches wide by 13 inches high and so would fit equally well on a desk, end table, book shelf, or room divider.

A pressed-flower switchplate adds an unexpected accent to a room.

Package tags like this one are easy to create from leftover and pressed flowers. In sets of a dozen they make delightful gifts. In red and green flowers they will be appreciated at Christmas package-wrapping time.

grows near the marshes, to subtly work the color of the basket into the arrangement.

Directly above the red peony, a blue hyacinth floret is visible. There are several in the arrangement that have been dried and wired individually. They add a nice, dainty look to the composition.

The tiny white flowers with yellow centers and the pink puff-ball-type flowers are English daisies, which dry perfectly in silica gel.

Seven pink carnations have been used in the design, and there are five bleached Japanese iris pods.

To complete the arrangement, I added five stems of rosy beauty berries, some white furry pearly everlasting, tiny clusters of pale blue hydrangea florets, which had been air dried, and just a few sprigs of white and pink statice.

This arrangement, although it includes preserved materials from every season, is timeless and would look as appropriate in the fall as it would in the spring.

Pressed Flower Projects

If you have collected a good selection of pressed ferns, leaves, and flowers, there are many decorative items you will want to make for your home, for gifts, or both.

The illustration shows a glass switch-plate I have decorated by gluing pressed materials to the glass.

The figure plainly shows how to make place cards and package ties from pressed, natural materials. By this same method you could decorate match covers and tally cards for bridge games (see figure). Also, plain notepaper becomes exquisite when decorated with a bouquet of pressed flowers, and party invitations decorated with natural materials become keepsakes of the occasion.

Another project I enjoy doing with pressed flowers is decorating 3-by-6-inch or 3-by-9-inch foliating-type candles. You simply glue the pressed ferns, leaves, and flowers onto the candle in an attractive design using a thin, white craft glue. When the glue has dried, paint over each flower, extending a little beyond the edges of each bloom, with the glue. This will seal the flowers from dampness and firmly attach them to the candle. The glue will dry crystal clear. If you will dry-press a few flowers from a friend's wedding and decorate a white candle in this manner, you will have an unusual gift to present to the couple on their first anniversary. They may wish to use this candle only on their wedding anniversaries or when entertaining other couples on theirs.

Flower prints are a favorite project of pressed flower enthusiasts. To make a print, you will need the following:

Materials

an assortment of pressed flowers and leaves
an attractive frame with glass

a piece of black, pale blue, or other color velvet or burlap, a little larger than the backing cardboard that comes with the frame

a tube of silicone tub sealer, clear

pointed tweezers

an artist's brush

toothpicks

masking tape

Instructions

1. Have your selection of pressed flowers ready to work with.

2. Cover the cardboard backing with the velvet, burlap, or other appropriate fabric by gluing at the corners and edges only. Pull the fabric tight and weight it down with a book until the glue sets. Use silicone sealer sparingly.

3. Arrange the flowers on the background material by carefully placing them in a design of your choice, using tweezers. Move them around with the bristles of the brush until you are quite satisfied with their placement.

4. Using a small amount of silicone sealer on a toothpick, apply it to the flowers as they remain in the design you have chosen.

5. When you have completed the flower print, place the glass over it and let it set overnight.

6. If you are not satisfied with the design the following day, add a few more leaves or flower petals to the arrangement, until you are satisfied with it. Then place the print into the frame and seal it around the back of the frame with masking tape to keep it airtight.

7. If you use an all-flat design such as this one, we refer to it as a print because it resembles a wallpaper or tapestry print.

8. If you use a shadow-box frame, you will be able to make a three-dimensional flower design using little pea-sized lumps of silicone sealer to elevate some of the flowers. Because silicone tub sealer contains no water, it is safe to seal your design as soon as you are satisfied with it. If you were to use a white craft glue for your pressed flower work, it would be necessary to wait until the glue dried thoroughly before sealing a design under glass. Otherwise, the water in the glue would wilt the flowers.

Candle Lantern

My favorite thing to do with pressed flowers, ferns, and leaves is to make candle lanterns. In the fall I enjoy collecting and drying colorful leaves and then making some lanterns of an assortment of autumn leaves. Using a sandalwood or cinnamon candle in the lantern and seeing the candlelight shining through the many colored leaves, creates a perfect setting for a lovely autumn evening at home, entertaining friends.

Sometimes I make candle lanterns of pressed spring wildflowers and ferns, and at other times my lanterns are made from a variety of brightly colored and pressed memories from my summer garden.

Again, trust me when I tell you the procedure is not difficult

A swirl of autumn leaves encased in "frosty" wax creates this glowing lantern. Only a tiny votive candle is needed to illuminate the dancing leaves.

and the results are electrifying.

To make a candle lantern (or three to nestle together), you will need the following:

Materials

>an assortment of pressed flowers, ferns, and leaves
>
>a clear glass or plastic container. The one in the sketch is 6¾ inches by 4½ inches. A smaller container could be a straight-sided Manhattan glass.
>
>white craft glue which dries clear
>
>small sheet of waxed paper, about 4 inches square
>
>votive candle
>
>white paraffin
>
>one 2-inch wide, clean paintbrush
>
>1 sheet of 8½-by-11-inch white paper

Instructions

1. Cover the work area with newspapers, and on the sheet of white paper, arrange the pressed flowers the way you would like to see them on the lantern. Try several patterns, moving the materials around until you are pleased with the design.

2. Working on the inside of the container, from the bottom upwards, the largest leaf or flower should be at the bottom. Dot the first leaf or flower you wish to glue with tiny dots of glue. Do not use more glue than necessary or it may take several days to dry.

3. With the piece of waxed paper, hold the flower firmly against the inside of the container until it adheres tightly.

4. Add the next flower or leaf and continue doing so until you have completed your design.

5. Set container aside to dry overnight.

6. When the white glue has dried, it should no longer appear white. That is when you can begin adding the paraffin.

7. Melt paraffin in an old coffee can seated in a pan of water. (*Never heat the wax in the can directly on the burner.*)

8. When the paraffin has reached the stage where it resembles clear water, remove the pan of water with the can of wax to a breadboard on your work table.

9. Holding your lantern container on its side, dip the brush into the melted wax and paint the floor inside of the container.

10. Next, dip the brush into the melted wax and, starting at the floor of the container, paint a strip of wax over a row of glued flowers, painting all the way to the top of the container.

11. The next brushful of wax should paint a second strip of wax from the bottom of the container to the top, alongside and slightly overlapping the first strip.

12. Continue painting strips of wax from the floor of the container to the top until the entire inside wall of the container is white with wax.

13. Coat the entire inside of the container with a second coat of wax. Light a candle inside of the lantern and if you detect any bare spots, fill them

in with wax. It is important to not make the wax coatings too heavy, or the light will not glow through to illuminate your leaves and flowers.

14. If you place a votive candle in its little glass holder inside the lantern and light it, you will have what appears to be a large, chubby candle or lantern, glowing and showing off your pretty flowers and leaves. Place a spoon of water in the votive candle holder so the flame will automatically extinguish itself when the candle burns down and thus prevent cracking the glass.

When making lanterns of autumn leaves, you can add a pretty touch by using pale blue wax instead of white. The blue will resemble the blue fall sky between the leaves without distorting the color of the leaves.

Now that you have seen how easy it was to make your candle lantern, why not make several more for friends, for the foyer, the powder room, the guest room, or your bedroom. Floral scented candles are especially nice with spring and summer flower lanterns.

SUMMER

Almost anywhere you might stop on a day in the country, on an afternoon at a lake, or on a vacation trip you can collect some unique natural materials which will add interest and pleasant memories to your winter bouquets and dried arrangements.

It is a common error to wait until late fall to begin collecting materials. If you do, you will lose out on many choice items. By collecting at *all* times of the year, you will soon develop an enviable assortment of pods, weeds, mosses, lichen, shells, driftwood, rocks, and other wildlings to choose from when you are ready to create.

Many cones drop in midsummer and so it is best to collect them at that time when their light beige and brown tones are fresh, and before they become discolored by fall rains or covered by autumn leaves. Seed pods collected in summer, while they are still green, retain their fresh, green coloring. In the fall you may collect seed pods from the same shrub, tree, or plant after they have turned a rich brown. Crape myrtle pods are a good example. A nice gradation of color from green to dark brown may be obtained by collecting materials at different stages of development.

Nuts may also be gathered in various stages of growth for variation in size and appearance. Husks of horse chestnuts, hickory nuts, pecans, and hazelnuts are quite effective in fall arrangements, on pine cone wreaths, in cone and pod baskets, and on wall plaques made of dried natural materials.

Sometimes you may have to race the squirrels to add to your nut collection. As early as August these furry little creatures are busy in our garden, disconnecting every hazelnut on our ancient, huge nut bush, and littering the lawn with them. The winged husks are still green on the nuts, so I save them for dried arrangements, but I can't help wishing that *some* could remain on the bush till maturity.

Summer is undoubtedly my busiest season. It is necessary to check the garden daily for perfect blooms to preserve in silica gel as the buds unfold. There are wildlings to gather at several stages of development and color that must be air dried. Time simply evaporates like steam as I check the plants for insects and mildew, and try to keep up with the weeding, feeding, and watering of the gardens. And, speaking of watering the garden, soaker hoses will do the job most efficiently. Keep the water pressure low so the ground is soaked but the water does not reach the flowers. *Never* sprinkle the garden overhead or you will end up with preserved flowers that are covered with brown splotches (water stains) that will only become apparent once the flowers are dried.

Although summer activities for the flower preservationist are many they are also joyous, for few accomplishments can equal the satisfaction found in saving beautiful flowers and other perishable plant material for enjoyment all year through.

Spanish Summer Patio Display

Wall arrangements show up where you least expect to find a flower display. In a kitchen, dimly lit hallway, on the front door, or in a recreation room where a conventional arrangement might be accidentally upset, a wall-type arrangement adds a colorful touch to an area that might otherwise go undecorated.

The container for the wall hanging I have designed resembles the wrought-iron grillwork of Mexico and Puerto Rico. It was made from a sisal placemat, which I folded up from one end, to form a pocket for the flowers. The pocket is held in place with stem wires twisted through the mat. (See figure.) Then the entire mat — back and front — was sprayed with black paint.

When making this arrangement, it is best to hang the container on the wall where it will be used to give you a better perspective as you work. Trim a block of floral foam to fit into the pocket, extending 3 inches above it. Pin the moss to cover the foam *before* it is glued into the pocket. The filler is German statice and silvery artemisia.

Because the container looks very Spanish to me, the flowers I chose are bold and bright. The focal point is an almost iridescent, red-crested celosia. Smaller pieces of this same variety of celosia carry the color throughout the design. Yellow helichrysums and vivid purple statice add to the Spanish flavor of this composition. For a finishing touch, blue hydrangea, shiny black jet beads, and a nosy monarch butterfly tie it all together.

Sea Lavender Tree

This sea lavender tree could be just the right gift for a "man-who-has-everything" and loves the sea, a former avid fisherman who no longer can make the trip to the seaside, or for grandparents who used to have a cottage by the sea. Such happy memories it could revive.

Materials

driftwood or other flat plank

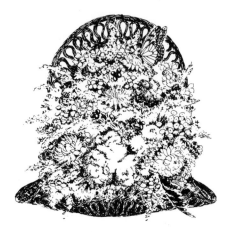

The container for this arrangement is a sisal placemat, spray-painted black to resemble wrought iron. If you use a different type of natural reed placemat, you may wish to make a similar container for a kitchen or dining room wall arrangement to match.

This sisal placemat looks very much like wrought iron when spray-painted black. Notice how the wire loops at the front help form a pocket.

This would make a lovely gift for someone who loves the sea and sand and seagulls.

block of floral foam

moss (gathered at the seashore)

sea lavender (gathered in the salt marshes in August or September, or purchased from a seaside florist)

aqua blue gypsy broom

aqua blue hill or starflowers

large yellow "Billy Buttons" from Australia (or similar sunny-colored material such as yellow daisy centers, yellow Spanish clover, or floral buttons)

assortment of seashells and tiny crabs found on the beach

seagull ornaments (purchased in craft shop)

stem wire

wire cutters

hot glue and glue gun, or thick white craft glue

cotton balls

Instructions

1. Glue brick of floral foam to the driftwood plank, more to the left side of the plank, allowing some wood to show at the right-hand side. Cover foam completely by pinning moss all over it.

2. Sea lavender is rather light and airy, so gather little bunches of it together in your fingers, until it assumes some substance, then push the bunched stems into the foam. As you insert the bunches of sea lavender into the foam, be conscious of the tree *shape* you are trying to form. It should be narrower at the top and wider at the base. If the top seems too wide, compress the moss-covered foam between your hands to make it narrower and rounder.

3. Once you have created your sea lavender tree, add sprigs of aqua-colored gypsy broom in a random pattern to suggest sky and sea. Also add the aqua hill or starflowers in the same manner.

4. The large Billy Buttons on my tree represented sunshine. If your supplier does not have these, any pretty, sunny yellow material will do.

5. At this point, tuck little tufts of glue-soaked cotton into the shells to be attached to the tree. Then insert stem wire into the cotton and set the shells aside to dry in an upright position (a glass tumbler will do).

6. When the glue is dry, attach shells to the tree by inserting the stem wire into the foam. Place large shells toward the bottom, smaller shells toward the top.

7. The seagulls come already stemmed, so simply insert them where they look best. The tiny crabs may be glued directly to the tree, as they are very lightweight.

8. I have tucked some seaside moss around the base of my tree for added interest.

I know this will look lovely in your family room, but didn't you make this one for grandpa?

Nesting Quail Arrangement

This little 6-inch basket arrangement hanging on the wall is a real conversation piece. It is easy to make for your home or for gift giving.

Materials

    1 oval or round basket, without a handle, 6-inch

    assortment of dried, natural materials, such as ferns, Indian paint-brush, millet, pearly everlasting, rabbit-foot clover, or peppergrass moss

    1 yard gingham ribbon, green

    1 feathered quail ornament (available at craft stores)

    stem wire, 6-inch

    wire cutters

    thick white craft glue

Instructions

1. Run the stem wire through a section of basket at the back where it won't show. Twist wire into a loop to form a hanger.

2. Make a bow, and glue it to the front top of the basket rim.

3. Glue small piece of moss into the basket to serve as a nest.

4. Glue the quail into the basket, facing out and toward the front edge.

5. Begin gluing your dried material into the basket, starting at the back with the tallest pieces. Any dried materials can be used for this design, the main idea being to create a natural, cozy, woodsy area where a quail might choose to nest or hide. I usually glue some little berries near the bird at the front of the basket and also a few hemlock cones to add interest. A little fluffy, Indian paintbrush around the bird would suggest a nest.

Giant Marigolds Basket Arrangement

This large, sturdy basket is the type in which fresh fruit gifts are packed. Because of its heavy weave and strong lines, I chose to use the dramatic, king-size blooms of Burpee's Climax hybrid and Senator Dirksen marigolds. The Climax hybrids are so large that they are almost ball-shaped, and some blooms grow up to 5 inches across. The Senator Dirksen variety is a large broad-petaled, golden-orange flower that grows up to 4 inches across. Because of their size, you may have passed them up when drying other garden flowers in silica gel. The next chance you have, dry some of these showstoppers. They are a joy to work with, and the results are truly amazing. They will look as fresh when dry as the day you picked them.

To complement these large blooms I contrived some unusual globe amaranth branches. I selected birch branches with a delicate curve, and, using my hot glue gun, I attached twelve magenta globe amaranth heads around the birch branch, starting about 1 inch from the tip. I soon had nine conversation-piece floral stems to add to my arrangement of impressive marigolds.

The arrangement also includes nine of Burpee's Nugget hybrid marigolds. These are much smaller than the Climax and Dirksen varieties but are quite spectacular in their own right. They are the earliest flowering marigold, often producing blooms from seed in six weeks! The plants are covered all summer with 2-inch fluffy yellow

A nesting quail basket to hang on your wall. Several hanging in a group are real conversation pieces. Made from scraps of natural materials, each one looks different. It's a great gift idea.

double blooms, right up to a heavy frost. They are perfect for edging flower and vegetable gardens and for use in patio planters, and they would brighten any apartment balcony.

Materials

heavy-weave basket, 9-by-6-by-7-inch, not counting handle
brick of floral foam
moss
natural, white, and green gypsy broom
glycerinized fern
brown heather
assorted wild grasses
9 yellow Nugget marigolds
7 Climax and Senator Dirksen marigolds
7 branches contrived globe amaranth stems
white hydrangea
purple statice
hot glue and glue gun, or thick white craft glue
stem wire
wire cutters
floral tape

Instructions

1. Glue an entire brick of floral foam into the center of the basket endwise.

2. Cover the foam with moss pinned on with short pieces of stem wire bent into hairpin shape (see page 37).

3. Because of the heavy nature of the basket and to minimize the size of the container, I made the end the focal point, instead of the front, as is usually done.

4. Insert the green gypsy broom filler all over the foam to create a rounded effect. Keep some of the gypsy flower heads near the foam and extend others to the edges of the basket.

5. To give the arrangement body, insert the glycerinized fern deeply into the filler extending a few fronds upward and outward.

6. Add your tallest stems of feathery heather and graceful wild grasses to establish the height and width of the design.

7. If you have not already stemmed your largest marigolds, do so now. Because their stems are hollow, I like to coat a wire stem with glue and insert it directly into the natural stem stub. When the glue has dried, tape the wire with floral tape for extra support.

8. Place the largest marigolds into your arrangement, positioning them near the bottom front and lower sides of the design.

9. At this point, more wild grasses were added to the arrangement to continue filling it out and to increase the triangular outline of the overall design.

10. Add the sunny yellow Nugget marigolds toward the top and center and extend out to the sides.

As incredibly fresh as these marigolds appear, they have been thoroughly dried in preheated silica gel in the microwave oven. The magenta globe amaranth branches match the woven magenta design in the basket.

11. Insert the impressive globe amaranth branches into the foam in between the yellow and orange marigolds.

12. Glue white, air-dried stemless hydrangea clusters into the arrangement on the filler to lighten the background and to add a delicate, lacy touch to this design.

13. Glue purple statice to the filler wherever an accent is needed and tuck in white gypsy all over the design as a light finishing touch.

Your marigold arrangement will light up the room in which it is displayed and look for all the world as though it just arrived from the florist shop!

Wildlings Arrangement

In my travels, I am always looking for unusual vases and bases for my arrangements. My friend Kris found this one for me in Mexico. It is made of lava ash clay.

The Mexican artist who created this lovely vase from natural, black lava ash clay, made it even more unusual by giving it just three legs and by decorating it with an open, cut-work band of flowers. This arrangement is a floor design that would look well year-round in a suitable corner of a large room or foyer.

The arrangement is quite large and looks impressive on the buffet in front of a large mirror. Almost all materials are wildlings and have been air-dried.

At the very top is a spire of bells of Ireland. Two more of these are at the bottom left and right side of the vase, forming a triangle. The silver-colored curly leaves are cecropia, found on El Yunque (a rain forest mountain in Puerto Rico) and also grown in south Florida. The flat brown leaves are souvenirs of my stay in the Virgin Islands, and the fluffy Indian paintbrush, wild white yarrow, golden tansy, brown feathery heather, and nigella pods were gathered here in southern New Jersey. The dark brown woody "flowers" were contrived from cotton pods. You can make some of these pretty posies by breaking the petals from several cotton pods, turning them over to their dark side, and gluing them around a central burr or small pine cone. Using a hot glue gun, you will soon have a nice array of these contrived flowers to add to arrangements or pine cone wreaths.

The bright orange material is from the Spanish bayonet plant. The orange part grows under the soil and requires washing before using. Pennycress and glycerinized leaves form the basic filler. A piece of floral foam, cut to fit the neck of the container, was wedged into it, extending 3 inches above the rim.

The dark brown spiny branches are acacia, and some golden acacia blooms are also used in this design. Peppergrass, wild oats, safflower branches, and clusters of crape myrtle pods complete this long-lasting design.

Tropical Arrangement

While completing this book at Bluebeard's Castle in the Virgin Islands, I gathered the woody pods and other materials which comprise this tropical arrangement. The base of the design is three round woven serving trays fastened together with hot glue. A large piece of floral foam is glued to the larger tray with hot glue to hold the heavi-

How nice to relive pleasant, happy times through reminders built into a flower arrangement. There could be no lovelier souvenir.

Nothing can brighten a dull winter day faster than a basket filled with brightly colored flowers. Friends will find it hard to believe that they were grown in your garden . . . last summer!

The excitement and charm found in the street markets of Rome and Paris are evident in this unusual market basket arrangement. It truly looks garden fresh due to the provincial container and close placement of the blooms in relation to each other, as well as the brightness of color and sheer number of flowers.

er background materials. A smaller piece of Sahara is glued into each of the two trays in the foreground. All foam was covered with moss and the flamboyant, ginger, frangipani, and other tropical pods, seeds, and grasses were added to create an arrangement filled with vivid memories of happy, peaceful days.

The rocks in the foreground are reminders of the surrounding mountains. The bright blue Spanish clover is reminiscent of the azure Caribbean sea and sky. The three candles in the hummingbird cups rekindle pleasant memories of the twinkling lights in the hills, dinners, and warm conversation with good friends. What more could you ask of an arrangement?

Zinnia Basket Arrangement

Baskets of flowers look as lovely in an office or hospital as they do in a home. The colors chosen for this arrangement are especially sunny and cheery. The zinnias and marigolds have been dried in silica gel, and the magenta globe amaranth, purple statice, and tiny cream-colored pyracantha blossoms were all air-dried. Also, if you look closely, you will see some yellow donkey-tail sedum blossoms that dried perfectly in silica gel and the microwave oven.

The main filler for the arrangement is green and white gypsy broom. The floral foam was fastened into the basket with hot glue and then covered with moss. The fillers were added in an overall pattern to form the circular shape desired. The zinnias, being the largest flowers, were added next. The rest of the flowers were placed, according to size and for pretty color distribution.

This type of arrangement would be nice to make for someone in a hospital or nursing home, because it is exceptionally bright and fresh looking, long-lasting, and needs no watering or other attention.

European-Style Basket Arrangement

One of the newest vogues in floral arranging today is the European style. It captures the freshness and vibrancy of the flowers found in the street markets of Paris and Rome. The flowers, rather than being arranged individually, are placed in a market-type basket to resemble the way the vendors display them. Masses of yellow flowers are together in bunches, then blue and violet ones. The red ones, all nestled together, make a crimson splash. The fresh-flower designer lines the basket with foil and uses water-soaked oasis to make this type arrangement.

I have used three blocks of floral foam in varying heights to give the flowers a cascading appearance. The foam was fastened into the container with hot glue and then covered with moss. The bright yellow and orange dried marigolds were then arranged very close together at the top of the arrangement. Usually in flower arranging, the idea is to allow plenty of "nodding room" between each flower head and to place the largest bloom at the bottom. The European-style market basket arrangement, however, requires just the opposite. The next section of flowers in this basket are lavender and purple statice (my souvenirs of the Tournament of Roses Parade in Pasadena, California). The lower level of flowers are dried zinnias and similar flowers that should be bunched together.

This type of arrangement is excitingly different from any dried arrangement I have ever tried. It can be an easy one for you to try, using a different variety of flowers if you wish. The main idea is to bunch masses of the same type of flower together for a striking color effect and to limit the groupings to three.

Colonial Five-Finger Vase Arrangement

This type of container is as popular today as it was during the colonial era. I suspect the main reason for its popularity is that it practically shapes the design for you. It is fan-shaped, and the center "finger" is taller than the end ones, so you know from the start that you will be making a triangular, one-sided design.

If your decorating taste is eighteenth-century Colonial, a fan-shaped arrangement of this type in a five-finger vase could look quite lovely on your mantel. Other containers appropriate for Williamsburg flower arrangements are jardinieres, Delft flower bricks, and baskets. The homemakers of Colonial Williamsburg also used common household items, such as porridge bowls, tea cups, mugs, and soup tureens.

Materials

    1 five-finger vase, 8-inch height
    sand for weighting vase
    5 small pieces of floral foam
    5 glycerinized magnolia leaves
    5 glycerinized ferns
    bridal wreath spires
    pink and blue delphinium spires
    goldenrod
    German statice
    red and yellow roses
    Queen Anne's lace
    purple statice
    yellow Spanish clover
    white mock-orange buds
    3 large coral-colored Lady Washington geranium florets
    lily of the valley foliage
    Vinca minor leaves
    silver dusty miller leaves
    5 wooden picks for magnolia leaves
    floral tape
    stem wire
    wire cutters

Instructions

1. *An important first step* in using this type of container is to fill it with dry sand or it will be top-heavy when completed. I then top off each "finger" with a piece of floral foam, firmly wedging it into the openings and allowing it to extend one inch above the rim of each opening. Do not cover the foam with moss, as the openings of the vase are so small that they will soon be

covered by the arrangement. Once you have readied your container, you are ready to begin.

2. I like to use glycerinized magnolia leaves for a background in this type of design, as they are sturdy and help "brace" the rest of the arrangement. (You may wish to use glycerinized fern, sumac, beech, or mahonia leaves.) Take time to wire and tape the stems of your background foliage, because there is only room in this container for *wire* stems. Thick, natural stems would soon have the tiny openings filled before your arrangement was finished. The background leaves in the center of this 8-inch-tall vase should reach 20 inches, which is two and a half times the height of the container. The leaves in the side "fingers" should be placed a little lower to form a triangle or fan shape. Place all stems in this arrangement as far back as possible, in order to conserve space.

3. Add glycerinized fern, bridal wreath, and pink and blue delphinium spires. Place the fern a little lower than the magnolia leaves to fill in the fan background. Place the delicate bridal wreath and delphinium spires to extend upward and outward.

4. Add goldenrod and German statice to give shape to the front of the arrangement. (You could also use plumed celosia pieces, heather, or silver artemisia for this purpose.)

5. From this point on, I worked from the top of the arrangement downward, carefully adding the red and yellow roses, Queen Anne's lace, purple statice, yellow Spanish clover, white mock-orange buds, and three large, coral-colored Lady Washington geranium florets. Wherever filler was needed to separate the flower heads, it was tucked in place. For the finishing touch, I glued foliage of the lily of the valley, *Vinca minor*, and dusty miller around the edges and in the center of the design. The addition of these leaves made the flowers look as though they had just been gathered from the garden.

An arrangement of this type looks especially lovely on a mantel or buffet. If you plan to display it in front of a mirror, be sure to finish the back neatly.

This lovely Morton stained-glass mirror kit went together with amazing ease. I chose an arrangement of pansies, wild cherry blossoms, mock-orange, lily of the valley, and hyacinth florets to complement the glass tones. The lily of the valley leaves (dried in the microwave oven) add a natural, fresh look to the overall design.

Pansies-and-Blossoms Mirror Display

This beautiful stained-glass mirror comes in kit form, manufactured by the Morton Glass Works of Morton, Illinois. The kit includes precut glass and a precut and finished walnut frame, a mirror, and truly easy-to-follow instructions. As soon as I saw it, I wanted to make an arrangement for the little shelf that would reflect in the mirror.

The brass planter that I chose for the container picks up the gold of the opaque glass.

Your arrangement could be any combination of early spring blossoms. The green leaves and spring green filler assure a springtime look. If you cannot find wild cherry blossoms, for example, the white German statice blossoms would give you a similar effect. Pussy willows would be delightful in this arrangement, as would short stems of bridal wreath. Candytuft could be used in place of the white hyacinth florets.

Materials

    assembled stained-glass mirror kit (see Sources)
    brass planter
    floral foam
    moss
    spring green and natural gypsy broom
    wild cherry blossom buds
    lily of the valley leaves and blossoms
    pansies
    blue ageratum
    white hyacinth florets
    mock-orange buds
    white pearly everlasting
    dusty miller leaves
    stem wire
    wire cutters
    scissors
    thick white craft glue

Instructions

1. Fit and glue a piece of floral foam into the brass planter, allowing 2 inches of floral foam to extend above the rim of the container.

2. Conceal foam by pinning moss all over it with stem wire bent into hairpin shapes.

3. Make a bed of spring green and natural gypsy broom, allowing it to extend over the rim of the planter about 2 inches.

4. Next, insert the tall woody stems of the wild cherry blossoms into the foam, placing them so they will reflect in the mirror on the left side of the arrangement. Place more of the wild cherry blossoms downward from that point and the rest of them to the far right, so that you have interspersed them into an *L*-shape.

5. Glue lily of the valley leaves all around the outer edge of the planter, making an attractive border. (The leaves should be dried in the microwave oven on a paper napkin.) Since you are working on a design to be placed close to a mirror, remember to keep the back rather flat.

6. Add the pansies next, since they are the largest flower.

7. Glue clusters of blue ageratum to the filler to save stemming time.

8. Add tiny white florets of the hyacinth, the mock-orange buds, and the delicate lily of the valley blossoms next, evenly distributing the white flowers throughout the arrangement.

9. Glue the pearly everlasting to the filler and a few dusty miller leaves in between the lily of the valley leaves.

The pansies look fresh enough for picking and the gold ones match the stained glass perfectly. Whenever I look at this arrangement throughout the year, spring and summer will suddenly return in my thoughts.

The warmth of candlelight, the beauty of flowers as fresh looking as the day they were growing in your garden . . . what lovelier centerpiece could you find for daily family dining or for festive occasions?

The large roses depict three large flowers glued in a triangular pattern. The zinnias show the next largest flowers glued in a triangular pattern between the largest blooms.

Candle Ring Centerpiece

A really impressive, yet simple-to-make arrangement is this candle ring centerpiece. (I designed this arrangement for the cover of *Crafts* magazine and have pictured it here with their permission.) As complicated as it appears to be, it goes together rapidly — all of the flowers are glued where they look their prettiest. What could be easier? You can use any combination of flowers. If you will be using the centerpiece in the spring rather than the fall, you might want to use light spring colors. If the candle ring will be the conversation piece on a fall table, lean more toward the gold and autumn tones.

Materials

1 floral foam preformed wreath base, 14-inch

moss

German statice

assortment of dried flowers such as roses, zinnias, cornflowers, hyacinth florets, marigolds, and delphiniums

pilar candle (optional: 3 thick, tall candles, usually foliating) 3-by-9-inch pilar or a brass or pewter candlestick with taper

stem wire

wire cutters

thick white craft glue

Instructions

1. The base of this arrangement is a 14-inch preformed ring. Pin moss all over it (except on the bottom) to create a natural or grassy-looking background. (See figure.) Then glue pieces of German statice to the moss in an even pattern so that a well-shaped bed is formed on which to arrange the flowers. The German statice helps to vary the height of each flower, making it appear as though they are growing in the arrangement.

2. Take the three largest flowers you have selected, and glue them to the wreath in a triangular pattern, using thick white craft glue.

3. Glue the three next-largest flowers in a triangular pattern in between the first three flowers. (See figure.)

4. Now here is some good news. There is no right or wrong way to finish your wreath. Simply glue the flowers in place where they look best, distributing the colors evenly. Use your smallest flowers for the finishing touches. Glue flowers only about three quarters of the way down the outside of the candle ring. This will leave the lower moss-covered edge to grip when moving the arrangement. The flowers, when glued in place, resemble a circular garden.

The candle I have used is a 3-by-9-inch gold one. To make it last longer, once it has burned down about 3 inches from the top, I inserted a votive candle. The votive candles can be changed as they burn down. Also, it is good to change the color of the large candle every now and then, giving the composition an entirely different appearance. A sky blue candle looks elegant with this candle ring as does brown, avocado green, or bittersweet. Perhaps you would like to coordinate the candle with the drapery or carpet color of the room in which it will be used.

Although this project uses many flowers, you will be able to dry them in just a short time if you use the microwave method described in this book. If your garden does not have enough variety of blooms, visit a nearby florist. Be sure to let the florist know that you will be *drying* the flowers, so will need the freshest ones he has.

Arrangement Under Glass

A beautifully preserved flower arrangement is not only made jewel-like by placing it under glass, but it is also protected from inquisitive fingers, dust, and humidity. My favorite under-glass-type container is the bell jar or dome, and it comes in many sizes with wooden, ebony, or metal bases. Other interesting glass containers are hurricane lantern globes (either vertical or horizontal), candy dishes, decorative jars and bottles, and crystal boxes.

The dome I have chosen for this summery arrangement is a 12-inch one with a walnut base. To add depth to the design, I glued a 2-inch-thick-by-3-inch-round piece of floral about two-thirds of the way back on the wooden base. Using stem-wire pins, I covered the foam with moss. I next inserted the tallest materials (sekko willow, eucalyptus, and bridal wreath) toward the back and sides of the design and established the highest point, checking often to make sure the dome would fit over the arrangement without touching it. Continuing the design, I positioned the light, airy materials on the upper and outer perimeter and the darker, larger flowers in the center and at the base of the design. Zinnias, blue delphinium, marigolds, German statice, helipterum, rose celosia, blue sage, purple statice, globe amaranths, and pyracantha blossoms complete this long-lasting arrangement. But all flowers look lovely under glass. For a friend who loves roses, a dome filled with perfectly preserved ones would be a year-round enjoyment. One of my favorite combinations is bridal wreath, the first luscious daffodils of the season, and grape hyacinths.

Silk and dried wedding and prom bouquets sealed in a dome are genuine conversation pieces and constant reminders of those very special days.

Once you are sure the arrangement is exactly the way you want it to remain, place the dome on it, *without* sealing it in place, and leave it overnight. You just may want to add one more flower or leaf the next day. For sealing the glass dome to the wooden base, I use clear silicone tub sealer. I also use silicone sealer when gluing flowers for placement under glass, as it contains no water that could ruin the dried flowers.

For a finishing touch, I glue a narrow, mossgreen velvet ribbon around the dome where it meets the wooden base.

A gift of flowers under glass will be treasured by the recipient for years. Although the bell jar reminds us of the Victorian era, an arrangement of this type would be appropriate in any setting.

AUTUMN

Right in the midst of a whirl of summer activities, without any warning, the evenings suddenly seem a little cooler, the air a bit crisper, and a certain kind of clear blue sky tells us that, unmistakably, autumn has arrived.

The gardens and meadows and marshes, which produced such a wealth of materials for drying in spring and summer, now offer different materials for collecting.

The wild, white yarrow has turned a rich, deep brown. The rosy green-tinged dock has turned to rust. The hydrangeas are no longer pink or blue, but their soft beige tones are very pleasing to see in fall arrangements in place of the usual fillers.

The pretty slate blue of the globe thistle (*Echinops ritro*) has faded, but the perfectly round head of this sturdy pod is an interesting shape to add to dried arrangements in either its natural beige or when bleached a snowy white.

The first week of August is best, in New Jersey, for gathering tightly budded Joe-Pye-weed. Its color is vivid when first in bud. The rest of the month, I gather it in varying stages of development, so that I am able to obtain flowers ranging from a bright rosy-lavender to a soft dusty mauve, all of the same material.

Mullein, those majestic tall spikes which seem to dominate the countryside in late summer and fall, fascinate me. I pick some when they are green and not yet so tall. In the fall I cut some of the spikes after they have turned brown. They are wonderful to use in fall arrangements because of their sturdiness, unusual shape, and delightful texture, comprised of hundreds of miniature woody flowers. I especially enjoy using mullein stalks in Christmas and Hanukkah decorations. For holiday designs I spray some a bright silver and some a red enamel. When spray-painted in white enamel and then over-sprayed lightly with silver, they resemble frosty icicles.

Simply gather the dry, brown spikes when they have been drying in the sun for several days. To make sure they are thoroughly dry inside, place them in a hot, well-ventilated attic or furnace room for several more days. Using colored candle wax to coordinate with the colors in the room where the fireplace is located, dip a dozen or more mullein stalks, 6 to 8 inches deep into the melted wax. (See Uses of Paraffin.) Hold each spike in an upright position until the wax solidifies on the mullein.

Displayed in a copper container with other tall dried materials, on the hearth, they can look quite decorative while waiting to be useful in starting your fires. During the holidays, stalks dipped in red wax can add to your holiday decor, and bundles of them tied with a festive ribbon will be appreciated by your friends. If the mullein is first sprinkled thoroughly with cinnamon before being dipped in the wax, it will fill the room with a spicy aroma when burned.

Late fall is the time to look for the starlike husks of beechnuts. These pods are unique in that they all drop from the tree at once following the first heavy frost. They should be collected immediately, before they become discolored and before they fall apart. Their tiny, wooden petals need reinforcing at the stem end, with a dot of hot glue or Duco cement to keep them intact. They may then be attached to wire stems for use as "wooden flowers" in an arrangement, or used without wire stems for decorative finishing touches to pine cone projects. Gather as many as you can, because this tree only produces nuts every *other* year.

Shapely branches of shrubs and trees may be collected in the late fall and winter when the leaves have fallen and it is easier to see the more desirable curved and angled branches and those encrusted with interesting lichen. Sweet gum (liquidambar), larch, birch, beechnut, oak, and dogwood are examples of trees that should be checked for use in arrangements. Thorn apple and acacia branches are good to add to your collection as are juniper branches dripping with their beautiful blue berries. If you pick juniper branches early, while the berries are white, you will have two different-looking materials to work with from the same source.

The luscious red coloring of the pomegranate makes it perfect for holiday decorations. I have used three small pomegranates on the woven wall tray on page 88. A centerpiece can be easily created just by placing dried pomegranates, dried artichokes, pine cones, assorted nuts, orange pyracantha berries, and rosy pepper berries on a shallow, woven straw tray in the center of your table. This combination of dried, natural materials has a definite fall appearance, which can be enhanced further by adding dried, colored fall leaves around the edge of the arrangement. If you sprinkle some cinnamon into one artichoke, some cloves into another, and some allspice into a third, the lovely centerpiece will even have a spicy, fall aroma.

To dry pomegranates some books advocate piercing the fruit to hasten the process, but I obtain excellent results by placing the pomegranates on top of my refrigerator without piercing them. To prevent the fruit drying with a flattened side, I turn it once each day. The

Decorative brooms are fun to create, use little material, and make delightful gifts. They can be used either indoors or out and are sure to make cheery any spot in which they are displayed.

pomegranates are dry when they become very lightweight.

In some cases you will want to glue these attractive fruits to a pine cone basket or wreath, and sometimes you will want simply to place them in a casual arrangement of dried materials and fruits for a centerpiece. If it becomes necessary to stem the pomegranate in order to include it in an arrangement, determine which is the prettiest side of the fruit and then insert a wooden pick into the fruit on the opposite side. Because the fruit is now hollow from drying out, the skin is easily pierced with the pointed end of the pick. I then remove the wooden pick, dip the flat end into thick white craft glue or hot glue, and reinsert it into the pomegranate.

Decorative Broom Display

It may surprise you to know that brooms are no longer used exclusively for witches' transportation or house cleaning. They are now decorated and hung on the fireplace, front door, kitchen door, or the wall in family rooms. Some are decorated in the holiday spirit complete with red velvet ribbon and jingle bells. Others are decorated in a spring motif with colored eggs and a nesting bird. The short-neck broom in this project was decorated in the rich golds and deep browns of autumn. You can use the following instructions to decorate any style broom, for any occasion or season.

Materials

    a broom
    small block of floral foam
    moss
    assortment of flowers such as gold helichrysum, purple statice, rust-colored immortelle, heal-all
    cones or pods
    green gypsy broom
    ribbon for bow, brown and orange plaid
    stem wire
    wire cutters
    scissors
    hot glue and glue gun, or thick white craft glue
    acrylic finish, clear
    acrylic spray, antique gold

Instructions

1. If your broom does not have a hanger, loop a piece of stem wire through the back at the handle and make a hanger loop.

2. Decide where you would like to build your arrangement on the broom. At that point, glue a block of floral foam about 4-inches square.

3. Pin moss on foam to conceal it, using pins made from stem wire.

4. Next decide the shape of your arrangement and insert background material in the foam to outline that shape. (I used foxtails for this.)

5. Add the bow at this point so that the arrangement can be built around it. By positioning the bow at this time, your arrangement will use less material.

6. Follow the foxtail outline, adding stems of heal-all or other spearlike material.

7. This is the time to add the green gypsy filler all over the foam, around the bow, and in between the bow loops, in a pattern somewhat like the rays of the sun.

8. Next, arrange the gold helichrysums, still following the original pattern outlined by the foxtails.

9. Now, glue heads of purple statice to the green gypsy, as a rich color accent.

10. Glue small clusters of rust-colored immortelles to the filler.

11. Glue a pretty protea pod to the center of the bow and add two more above and below the bow. Spray the pods with a clear acrylic finish and then lightly oversprayed with antique gold.

Brooms are fun to decorate because they are assembled with ease and make great gifts for housewarmings, showers, and that friend who has everything. One made especially for the kitchen wall could include cinnamon sticks, cloves, bay leaves, and other spicy-smelling materials.

Weed Wreath

This is a huge undertaking, but well worth the time and effort. The procedure is simple and easy, but to make a really effective wreath requires a variety of air-dried natural materials in abundance. When you hang your completed project over the fireplace, or on the wall in your family room, it will look as though you have brought the entire autumn season indoors, and it will give you pleasure for many years.

This wreath is made on a floral foam ring, 16 inches in diameter and 2 inches thick. A white styrofoam ring would also suffice. Using a piece of floral tape, I stretched it around the foam ring at the top. Taking a piece of stem wire, I wrapped it over the tape to form a hanger loop. The tape will keep the wire from cutting through the foam ring. (See figure.)

If you have been combing the meadows and fields and have squirreled away a good selection of dried natural materials, such as goldenrod, Joe-Pye-weed, heather, Indian paintbrush, tansy, wild yarrow, teasel, sumac, curly dock, Queen Anne's lace, peppergrass, pennycress, cat's paw, and sweet everlasting, you are ready to begin your wreath.

Materials

1 foam wreath ring, 16-inch

assortment of fillers: goldenrod, wild heather, Joe-Pye-weed, Indian paintbrush, pearly everlasting, curly dock, peppergrass, pennycress, sweet everlasting, and similar wildlings with which to build the shape of the wreath.

A rich blending of twenty-six varieties of air-dried wildlings were used to create this welcome-to-autumn wreath. If your color scheme leans toward the golds, browns, and oranges, it would be appropriate as a year-round accent piece.

assortment of special interest materials: Japanese lanterns, hydrangea, golden hybrid yarrow, dusty miller, cat's paw, Queen Anne's lace, crape myrtle blooms and pods, rhododendron pods, iris pods, jet bead berries, ageratum, globe amaranths, Yakima berries, teasel thistles, datura pods, and so on

1 red cardinal ornament (optional)

3 burlap ribbon bows, chocolate brown (optional)

acrylic spray, matte

floral tape

thick white craft glue

stem wire, about 6-inch

wire cutters

Instructions

1. Outline the entire wreath ring by inserting stems of goldenrod, heather, or another material of similar shape perpendicular with the surface of the foam ring. Each stem should extend out from the edge of the ring the same distance. This will determine how large your wreath will be. My finished wreath is 25 inches in diameter.

2. Insert the second row of stems in front of the first row and in between the stems forming the first row. Do not place the second row of stems directly in front of the first stems but slightly offset the second row.

3. Continue inserting a variety of dried materials in the wreath base, each row of stems being a little shorter than the previous row.

4. When you reach the outer ridge of the foam circle, change the direction of the stems you insert to a slight upward angle. As you go over that ridge, insert the stems almost straight up and down.

5. Hold the wreath out in front of you. It should be taking on a well-rounded appearance once you have filled in above the ridge. Continue adding filler of goldenrod, heather, or peppergrass (or your choice of similar material), until you have completely covered the sides and top surface of your foam circle. The stems inserted on the face of your wreath will be much shorter than the rest.

6. At this point go over the entire wreath, inserting sweet everlasting, pearly everlasting, and Indian paintbrush in order to "fluff out" the wreath and fill in wherever necessary.

7. It is now time to add the special interest items that will make your wreath come alive. If you plan to use the burlap ribbon bows and cardinal, add them at this time. You may use *any* assortment of air-dried materials on your wreath. Whatever you have the most of should be your filler for the main base of the wreath and to round it out. Save the unusual pods and flowers for decoration of the top and sides.

Any time you would like to freshen your wreath, simply spray it with a matte sealer or water-free hairspray, outdoors. You can add new material to it and even change the color of the bows over the years to give it an entirely different look.

I always add blue flowers to my fall-colored arrangements. I feel that the reason the colors of autumn look so exciting to us is that they are brightest when seen against a bright blue sky. In this wreath

The first step in making a wreath is to attach the hanger firmly.

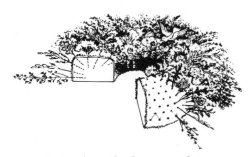

Notice how the first row of stems is inserted straight out from the wreath base and how the succeeding rows are inserted at a slightly upward angle.

the hydrangeas are my sky. If you cannot find hydrangeas in your area, blue ageratum or blue sage will air dry well and add a beautiful touch of sky to your wreath. If you do not have ageratum or sage in your garden a visit to a roadside nursery will solve the problem. Blue statice is another good choice and can be purchased at your local florist.

Did I hear someone say he is allergic to sumac and goldenrod? "Bet you're not!" Turn to Facts About Flowers for a pleasant surprise.

Topiary Tree

Originating in Greece, topiary displays reached a high art in seventeenth-century English gardens. Queen Mary concerned herself with raising exotic flowers, and her husband, King William, devoted much time and enthusiasm to topiary gardening. In many old paintings, topiary trees can be seen in the background, sometimes decorated with red apples. Around 1750, when the American colonists began to prosper, the art of "green sculpture" developed on this side of the ocean.

The topiary tree pictured here is not carved out of greenery, but rather is composed of everlasting fall flowers. Any assortment of stemless flowers can be used for this decoration. If you plan to make one for decorating your den, foyer, or family room in the autumn, you will find a good assortment of fall-colored flowers available in the shops. If you would like to make a topiary tree for use as a Christmas decoration, you will want to choose a red and green assortment of flowers, with a sprinkling of white ones as reminders of snow and frost. This type of arrangement also makes an unusual addition to a shower buffet if done in pink roses and carnations. It also makes a decorative centerpiece for a silver anniversary if the finished piece is sprayed with silver paint. Whatever your purpose in assembling a topiary tree, the basic instructions are the same—only the flowers covering the head will be different. In creating this design, allow yourself plenty of time. Make it a week or two in advance of the special occasion, if possible. (It will take a while for the plaster to harden and for the ball to dry.)

Neat and trim, a topiary tree can enhance a contemporary home, as well as one of Colonial decor. It's versatility is boundless as a seasonal design, shower, or party decoration, depending only upon the color scheme and materials used to construct it.

Materials

1 pound plaster of Paris

1 metal bowl, 6-inch

1 wooden dowel, ½-inch diameter, 15-inch length

1 styrofoam ball, 6-inch

sheet moss

7 heads of gold yarrow

assortment of everlasting flowers: such as helichrysum, purple statice, tansy, globe amaranth, German statice, hemlock cones, or other small pods

3 white pine cones

Arrangement Under Glass

Candle Ring Centerpiece

Decorative Broom Display

Pansies-and-Blossoms Mirror Display

Walnut Plank Spring Scene

Zinnia Basket Arrangement

Blue and Gold Hearthside Arrangement

Fantasy in Ice Arrangement

Gucci Ribbons Christmas Arrangement

Red Rose Valentine

*Silk and Dried Flowers
Wedding Bouquet*

*Maid of Honor's Bouquet and
Throwaway Bouquet*

Pine Cone Wreath

Madonna Garden Scene

Colonial Five-Finger Vase Arrangement

Contemporary Arrangement

Resplendent Duck Arrangement

Wildlings Vase Arrangement

Golden Yarrow Wreath

Tropical Arrangement

Spanish Summer Patio Display

Weed Wreath

European-Style Basket Arrangement

Pomegranate Wall Display

2 yards ribbon, 1-inch width, green gingham

15 inches velvet ribbon, 2-inch width, avocado green

newspapers

hot glue and glue gun, or linoleum paste

stem wire

wire cutters

Instructions

1. Cover work surface with newspapers.

2. Place plaster in 6-inch bowl. Add two-thirds cup of water to the plaster and stir with the dowel to mix thoroughly. Since plaster hardens *fast*, do not leave your project at this time. Continue stirring plaster until you feel it harden to the point where you can stand the dowel in an upright position in the center of the bowl. The dowel will be the trunk of your tree, so you want to make certain it is standing straight and is properly centered in the bowl. Set project aside to harden overnight.

3. When you are certain the plaster has hardened, make a small hole in the foam ball about 3 inches deep. Put some hot glue or linoleum paste on the upright end of the dowel and insert it into the foam ball.

4. Apply tufts of sheet moss to the ball with glue. Press the moss firmly in place as you work, to ensure a tight bond. This will be the foundation of your arrangement so it must be firm. Mold it with your hands to give it a nice, round shape.

5. Set project aside to dry overnight, so the weight of the flowers and glue to be added will not pull the moss loose.

6. The yarrow should now be arranged attractively on the topiary head by gluing the flower heads to the moss. Use enough glue to hold the yarrow tightly against the moss. Stand back and check the shape of your arrangement thus far. It should be well rounded.

7. Next, glue the assorted everlasting flowers to the head, paying special attention to the color distribution. It would not look right to have all the purple flowers on one side.

8. Add small pine cones, sprigs of German statice, and tansy in between the flowers to give an attractive finish to the arrangement.

9. Apply glue to dowel "trunk" of the tree and wrap your green velvet ribbon diagonally around it, from the head to the bowl. Hold it in place a few seconds until the glue dries or use a twist tie to hold it.

10. Glue moss to the plaster in the bowl, to conceal it. Glue white pine cones on end and tuck some pretty little flowers in around the cones.

11. Make a bow of the gingham ribbon and glue it to the front of the lower arrangement.

12. The metal bowl used as a base for your arrangement can now be placed into an attractive basket, wooden bowl, or other container.

Blue and Gold Hearthside Arrangement

This pretty hearthside basket is a souvenir of the Virgin Islands. It is shaped differently from most hearthsides, and the light-colored reed running through the handle reminds me of baby ribbon threaded through eyelet.

This light and airy hearthside basket design brings back memories of sunny, pleasant days in St. Thomas where I purchased the interesting basket. Like good books and warm friends, souvenirs of this type return happy thoughts for years to come.

Any hearthside basket will work well with this fall-colored design which features blue delphinium florets, three gloriosa daisies, golden coreopsis, Green Envy zinnias, gallardias, seaside goldenrod, heather, and a sprinkling of white gypsy broom. False Boneset *(Kuhnla eupatorioides)*, dipped in green alcohol dye and dried, is the filler and glycerinized fern deep in the arrangement adds body. In the foreground are several stems of wild cherry blossom buds, and airy peppergrass finishes the arrangement.

This design would look lovely on an end table or kitchen table, in the bedroom or family room. Being one-sided, it needs to be placed against a wall.

If sprayed with a clear acrylic sealer, this open basket of flowers should bring you much joy for many months.

Golden Yarrow Wreath

You will have sunshine throughout fall and all winter long wherever you place this golden yarrow wreath. It looks especially beautiful hanging on a dark walnut-paneled wall or near a glowing fireplace. If used indoors, it will last for many seasons as it is made of sturdy, woody materials. My wreath was constructed on a preformed floral foam base, 14 inches in diameter. For use directly over a fireplace, you might want to make a larger wreath, in which case a 16-inch base would work equally well for this design.

A wreath of golden yarrow, pheasant feathers, teasel, cones, and gilded milo berries (sorghum), will bring sunshine into any room in which it is displayed, all through the fall and winter months.

Materials

    foam wreath base or any white styrofoam base, 14-inch diameter
    moss
    golden yarrow
    teasel (sprayed October-brown)
    5 pheasant feathers
    assortment of pine cones
    ribbon, in autumn-toned plaid
    black-eyed Susan centers or other round-shaped, brown dried material
    milo
    newspaper
    stem wire
    wire cutters
    hot glue and glue gun, or thick white craft glue
    scissors
    floral tape
    acrylic spray, gold
    acrylic spray, clear

Instructions

1. Cover work area with newspaper.
2. Wrap a piece of floral tape around the wreath at the top. (See figure, page 73.)

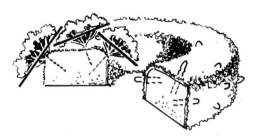

Pin moss to the foam wreath base with fern pins or little hairpin shapes made of stem wire.

The left side of this illustration shows the angles to use and how to attach the heads of yarrow to the wreath.

3. Run a stem wire over the tape so that both ends of the wire will be above the wreath. The tape will prevent the wire from cutting through the foam.

4. With both wire ends above the wreath, twist them together to hold the wire in place and then twist the ends into a loop for hanging the wreath.

5. Place foam wreath on newspaper and pin tufts of sheet moss to it with stem wire bent into hairpin shape. Conceal entire foam surface—sides and front—with moss. Make sure moss is fastened securely. (See figure.)

6. Cut the stems from all the yarrow heads, leaving a stub of about 1 inch.

7. If you are using a hot glue gun, the next step will go rapidly. If you are using thick white craft glue, you may have to allow time for the glue to set.

8. Glue one head of yarrow on the wreath base, near the center opening (inner rim), at the top of the wreath.

9. Glue another head of yarrow to slightly overlap the first head. (See figure.) Add a third head overlapping the second one.

10. Continue gluing yarrow to the wreath base in this manner, two-thirds of the way around the foam circle, checking the illustration often.

11. Add the brown teasel by inserting their strong stems into the foam, as illustrated.

12. Insert five pheasant feathers into the foam, extending off the edge of the wreath at various angles.

13. Wire the medium-sized pine cones to wooden picks and insert them into the design to fill between the teasel and to form a center.

14. Glue loops of autumn-colored plaid ribbon into the arrangement and add three ribbon streamers to the lower left side of the wreath, extending downward at different levels.

15. The round brown pods are the centers from black-eyed Susans. Overspray them lightly with gold paint, and glue them into the arrangement at jaunty angles.

16. Glue the little clusters of gilded berries (milo that have been sprayed gold) in place wherever they are needed to separate the browns and make the design come alive.

17. Cut a 6-inch piece of ribbon and fold it to make a loop. Staple the two ends together. Dip the ends in glue and insert them into your arrangement. The loops are every bit as pretty as bows, using lots less ribbon.

Ribbon loops may act as fillers in wedding table arrangements, holiday designs, and prom and wedding bouquets.

Resplendent Duck Arrangement

What a welcome gift this little duck would be for an outdoorsman, sportsman, or male friend in the hospital. It would look equally at home in an office, especially in the fall. One of the joys of a dried floral arrangement is that it doesn't require sunshine and water. For this reason it is especially welcomed by men and women who lack "green thumbs" or have enough to keep them busy at the office without tending to plants.

Ducks are so appropriate as gifts for outdoorsmen. This one, carrying a special arrangement, will last for years.

Materials

    duck planter (available at garden centers and floral-supply shops)

    1 brick of floral foam

    moss

    German statice

    green, brown, and white gypsy broom

    7 stems of wheat or barley

    assortment of fall-colored natural materials

    7 stalks of barley

    thick white craft glue

    stem wire

    wire cutters

Instructions

1. Glue floral foam into duck cavity.
2. Cover foam with moss pinned with stem wire hairpins.
3. Outline the floral foam with German statice to make a border.
4. Create a bed of green gypsy broom in an overall pattern to cover the foam. This is an "all around" type of circular arrangement, so you want it to look equally well from any angle.
5. Next insert seven stems of wheat or bearded barley. By placing one in the center of the arrangement, you will establish the height of the design. The ones on either side of the duck's neck, out the sides of the arrangement, and above its tail suggest feathers.
6. You may fill in the arrangement with any type of dried material you have been preserving. I used little clusters of golden tansy, gold starflowers, blue Yakima berries (viburnum berries would be a good substitute), and rust-colored dudinea from Israel. Also I added a tiny bit of rust gypsy to extend the rust color throughout the design.

Although the colors of this design are appropriate for the fall season, if the carpet, draperies, and upholstery of the room in which it is placed lean to the golds, browns, and rusts, it could be considered a year-round arrangement.

Bread Loaf Bouquet

A flower arrangement made in a loaf of dried, varnished bread is a real conversation piece and adds a decidedly "country flavor" wherever it is used. The country-look is definitely "in" and promises to be popular for some time to come because of its warmth and comfortable coziness. An arrangement in a loaf of bread is exceptionally attractive when displayed on a checkered tablecloth.

Materials

    1 loaf of bread (your choice of round, long Italian, or French)

    acrylic sealer, matte

    ¼ brick of floral foam

    moss

A loaf of bread, dried and varnished, makes an unusual container and conversation piece. It is especially appropriate for a bread-and-butter gift, for centerpieces at a picnic or barbecue, or for a housewarming.

assortment of flowers, such as carnations, Yakima berries, and celosia

filler of your choice, such as German statice, gypsy broom, or broom bloom

sharp knife

stem wire

wire cutters

hot glue and glue gun, or thick white craft glue

Instructions

1. With a sharp, pointed knife cut into the loaf at the top, at an angle, allowing a one-inch wall all around the loaf. In other words, do not cut too close to the sides of the loaf lest they cave in while drying. Cut from one end of the loaf to the other. Then turn the loaf around and cut from one end to the other on that side of the bread. Leave a one-inch floor to your "container," too.

2. At this point, you should be able to lift the heart of the loaf out in a *V* shape. This makes a delicious lunch — a little difficult to make a sandwich with, but perfect for fondue or rarebit.

3. Place the bread on a trivet on top of the refrigerator. The heat from the motor will dry the loaf in just three to four days.

4. When you are sure the bread is thoroughly dry, varnish it with several coats of acrylic sealer inside and out.

5. You now have a unique container in which to construct your flower arrangement (or to line with a gingham napkin and use for serving breadsticks or crackers). To make the flower arrangement in the bread, shape a piece of floral foam to fit into the opening and to extend one inch above the edge of the container. Glue the foam into the dried bread either with hot glue or thick white craft glue.

6. You are now ready to pin moss on the foam to conceal it, add a filler of gypsy broom or German statice, and complete your design. Any combination of flowers works well with this unusual container. I have used carnations, Yakima berries, and celosia in the arrangement sketched. Helichrysums and other fall-colored flowers look especially nice in the bread base.

This arrangement created in a round loaf of bread makes a charming centerpiece for a dining table. Arrangements constructed in long loaves of bread are perfect as one-sided designs for the back of a buffet. Using these same general instructions, Kaiser rolls can be converted into interesting cardtable centerpieces, for special themes such as St. Patrick's Day or Valentine's Day.

Holiday Cones and Pods Basket

To make a basket arrangement of pine cones and woody pods, you will need an assortment of cones, I like to have ten to fifteen white pine cones or Norway spruce cones handy when making basket arrangements. As they are long and easily matched in size, they make a nice, even edging to the arrangement. You may refer to the illustration as a guide in helping you construct your basket arrangement, but remember that this is your own personal creation. Place the cones and pods where they look prettiest to you.

Materials

  princess basket, 8- or 10-inch

  assortment of pine cones and pods in varying shapes and sizes

  rose hips (optional)

  ribbon of your choice

  newspaper

  linoleum paste

  wire cutters or pruning shears and clippers (optional)

  glossy acrylic spray, clear

  small paintbrush

Instructions

1. Cover the work area with newspaper to avoid getting paste and sticky sap on the table. Take a sheet of newspaper and form it into an oval-shaped roll about the size of a baking potato. Tuck all the ends of the paper inside the roll in order to make a hard, solid foundation on which to build your cone arrangement.

2. Spread linoleum paste thickly on the bottom of the paper core and hold it firmly in the center of the basket for a few minutes (or weight it down with a saucer).

3. While the glue is setting, sort your cones and pods into small, medium, and large sizes. Once the paper core is firmly anchored in the basket, dip the stem ends of your long cones in the paste and glue them to the paper core. The open ends of the cones should extend slightly over the edge of the basket, forming a nice border, and the middle of each cone should be flat against the bottom of the basket.

4. Next, work with your medium-size cones and glue them in between the long cones, using about a teaspoonful of paste on each one. Cones glued on the left side of the arrangement should be facing slightly to the left, and cones placed on the right side of the arrangement should be facing slightly toward the right. I find my arrangements look best when I keep them centrally balanced. I accomplish this by placing a cone on the right side of the design and then placing a similar cone exactly opposite on the left side. If I place a certain pod at the top of the arrangement, I place another one directly below at the bottom of the arrangement. Decide which of your cones is the most unusual and largest. The largest cone or pod should always be at the center, toward the bottom, for good balance. Glue this special cone in place now, so the rest of your design can be built around it. If you do not have a special cone that you would like to use for a focal point, see Step 5.

5. (Optional.) If you would like to make a pine cone flower for the focal point, it is easier than you might think. Simply choose a large pine cone, and, with the help of a sharp pair of pruning shears or wire cutters, you will soon become an expert. Hold the cone firmly in one hand while you force the open cutters into the cone as far as they will go between the pine cone petals, three or four rows up from the bottom of the cone. Cut with the clippers. Do not try to cut through the cone with this first cutting or the flower may fall apart. Move the clippers around to the opposite side of the cone and make another cut. On very large cones you may have to rotate the cone, making four or five cuts, before the cone will separate giving you a zinnia-type flower. The white pine cone is the easiest to cut and will give you pretty "flowers" edged in brown. These can be used in your basket arrangement, or stemmed and used

The principles used in creating this table top pine cone basket can also be used to make large hearthside baskets to decorate your hearth or to fill the fireplace during the times when it is not in use.

in a dried floral arrangement. A cluster of three of these would make a nice focal point for your basket in the event you did not have a larger cone with which to make your centerpiece.

6. Continue building your woody arrangement by gluing one cone on top of another, trying to keep the design balanced, and finish by gluing the smallest cones and pods on top of the arrangement. Wherever you have a little gap to fill, insert a small cone or pod.

7. You will note I have added a red-and-white checked bow to my basket and have glued red rose hips between the cones to give the basket a holiday flavor. You may wish to leave your basket unadorned and thus make it appropriate for use year-round.

8. Spray your pine cone arrangements with a clear glossy acrylic spray to bring out the many different shades of wood and to make the arrangement easier to clean. To freshen your design, dust with a small paintbrush and then respray lightly with the acrylic spray.

This type of basket arrangement makes a lovely decoration for any room of your home and makes an especially welcome gift. By using the same technique, you may wish to make a hearthside basket for your fireplace. A 22- or 24-inch basket filled with cones and pods looks quite elegant on the hearth, especially during the holidays. Shiny red Christmas tree balls and sprigs of holly can be inserted between the cones. When the holidays have passed, the balls and holly are easily removed, and the cone basket can continue to be enjoyed year-round. In the summer when the fireplace is no longer in use, the basket of cones can be placed in the fire area. Fresh magnolia or rhododendron leaves or evergreens can be tucked among the cones for a fresh look. When they dry out, they can be easily replaced.

Summer Memories Arrangement

How nice it is to be reminded of the warmth and fun of summer while the winter wind is howling and the chill is in the air. This arrangement uses very few materials and goes together quickly. If you were a diligent shell collector last summer (and there is usually one in every family), you are ready to begin. The shells for this design are from my son Craig's collection.

Materials

shallow planter (white with aqua lining would be nice)
floral clay
lid from spray can
figurine of a child or children
several small rocks
bare branches, such as birch or beech
3 seagull ornaments
small amount of sea lavender
assorted seashells
aquarium gravel, white
small shell for candle (or substitute votive candle in glass holder)

This Summer Memories arrangement includes its own little beach, some shells, water, seagulls, and a few natural branches. The child holding a bouquet of sea lavender and shells might represent your own childhood by the sea. The tiny floating candle adds warmth.

Instructions

1. Soften floral clay in hands until pliable. Press a piece of it, about the size of a half dollar onto the back, left side of the planter. This will be used to hold the bare branches. Do *not* flatten it out, but press it to the dish in lump form.

2. Soften more floral clay and press it on the bottom *rim* of a spray can lid in a strip. Fasten the lid to the shallow container, just in front of the first lump of clay.

3. Soften more clay, enough to cover the bottom of the figurine you are using. Press the piece of clay to the base of the figurine *in lump form* and then press the figurine to the top of the spray can lid. As you press down on the figurine, the clay on its base will spread out giving you a good bond.

4. Locate some rugged-looking rocks from outdoors. Use floral clay to fasten them around the base of the figurine (the spray can lid) to conceal it.

5. Next, cut some bare branches to a good height for your figurine and insert the stems into the first lump of clay, which you attached to the side bottom of the shallow dish. Angle them so they will look graceful and airy behind the figurine. Refer to the illustration for an idea of how to arrange your branches.

6. Glue the three seagulls to the branches as though they just alit.

7. If there are hands showing on the figurine, press a small piece of clay to the hands and press on a small piece of moss to cover the clay. Insert tiny sprigs of sea lavender into the clay to form a bouquet in the hands of the figurine. Glue short stem wire pieces to the tiniest seashells and attach them to the bouquet.

8. Arrange seashells in an attractive manner around rocks and figurine and anchor them firmly with bits of clay.

9. Add the white aquarium gravel by the spoonful in between the shells and rocks and around the base of the tree branches. With the gravel form a small beach around the base of the rocks.

10. Attach three white pebbles in the right front of the shallow container to hold a seashell candle. My candle was made by filling a shell with melted paraffin and adding a wire core wick. As a substitute, you could stand a votive candle in a glass holder, where I attached the white pebbles.

11. The last step is to *gently* fill the shallow dish with water, using a spouted, houseplant watering can, in order not to disturb the placement of the gravel. Make the water as deep as possible, so that it will be an effective part of the seaside scene. The water will also add humidity, which your heating system has probably removed from the air in your home.

Nothing to do now but sit back and admire your handiwork and mentally review those barbecues, fishing trips, ocean dips, and the fun of last summer.

The tree of bare branches, which you created for the seagulls in this arrangement, could add a lovely background to another design, if, instead of seagulls, you were to glue silk blossoms or dried globe amaranths, tiny hemlock cones, helichrysums, or ammobiums to the branches.

Floral branches of this type look especially nice in spring arrangements. The trunk of the spring blossom tree should be inserted

The simplicity of an oriental design is both pleasing to the eye and easy to construct. In this arrangement I have glued silk blossoms to natural branches. Blossoms dried in silica gel may also be attractively displayed this way, and pink or white helichrysums glued to these branches would have been equally attractive.

Dogwood blossoms dried in preheated silica gel or the microwave oven can be glued to natural branches to make this fresh-looking arrangement. Glycerinized magnolia leaves add interest to the foreground.

Wreaths of this type can be enjoyed every day of the year because they resemble an interesting wood carving. They can add a special touch of elegance to a den or family room and they last indefinitely.

into a base of floral foam, which has been glued into position on a wooden base, in a shallow dish or a vase.

The illustration shows a good example of how this type of arrangement can be truly elegant. I used hot glue to attach each blossom to the branches. (Thick white craft glue would have worked equally well.) By removing the silk blossoms from their wire stems and gluing them to natural stems they take on a quite believably fresh and natural appearance.

Bare, natural tree branches, such as birch, beech, and dogwood, enhanced with silk or dried flowers, also add a light touch to arrangements made in a vase. They can sometimes be used to carry the eye higher in a tall arrangement, where other materials might cause the design to look too heavy. (See figure.)

Pine Cone Wreath

In America we tend to relate wreaths only to the Christmas season. But wreaths are a symbol of eternal life and were used centuries ago by the Egyptians, Hebrews, Romans, and Chinese. When displayed with imagination and combined with other materials, pine cone wreaths become more than a Yuletide decoration. They add an exquisite decorative accent to a den, office, library, or recreation room, year-round.

The more varied the pods and cones are in shape, size, and wood tone, the more interesting will be your wreath. So, before undertaking this project, you may want to spend several seasons collecting, drying, and conditioning a supply of these materials. Vacation trips and visits to the park and seashore provide excellent opportunities for adding to your collection. For truly unusual cones and pods from all over the world, Curtis-Woodard (see Sources) is my favorite mail-order source.

While building up your supply of cones and pods, be sure to gather more than you think you will need because you *will* need more. As soon as friends see your wreath, they will want you to make one for them.

A pine cone wreath is not difficult to make, but it does take a lot of time. There are several methods that can be used. The one I feel creates the sturdiest wreath is the one made on a wire-box wreath frame with triple wire ring. This may be purchased at a floral- or garden-supply or craft store. My wreath was made on a 14-inch frame.

Materials

1 wire-box wreath frame, triple ring, 14-inch (available at craft stores and garden centers)

46 or more white pine cones (number depends on their size) or 46 Norway pine cones

assortment of round cones, such as loblolly, Scotch pine, ponderosa, and pitch pine

assortment of exotic cones, such as hakea, eucalyptus, casuarina, protea, lotus, agave, aulax, leucadendron, and cedrela

rhododendron pods

a feathered quail ornament (optional)

assorted dried fruits (optional)

linoleum paste or hot glue

1 role of wreath wrap wire (available at craft stores and garden-supply
centers)

1 can glossy acrylic spray, clear

wire cutters

pruning shears

Instructions

1. Pack the bottom layer of the wire ring tightly with white pine cones,
side by side. The white pine cone is slender, has white-tipped petals, and is
easy to crush. By pressing the cones together, very tightly, you might fit for-
ty-six into the ring. When doing this step, try to have the white pine cones
extend the same distance over the outside edge of the frame. You now have a
strong base on which to build your wreath. (If you live in the area where
white pine cones are scarce, you may be able to find the slender cone of the
Norway pine. The petals of this cone are tougher than the white pine and are
not crushable. To use these cones in a wreath frame, soak them in warm
water until they close up. This usually takes ten to fifteen minutes. Once they
are closed, they will slip into the bottom layer of the box wreath frame, easily. Pack them tightly, side by side, and set the wreath in the sun to dry. As the
cones dry, they will expand forming a tight, sturdy base on which to build the
rest of your wreath.)

2. At this point, I like to decide which shall be the top of the wreath. I
attach a strong wire hanger at the back where it will not show. Your wreath
will be quite heavy when dry, so be sure your hanger is sturdy.

3. There are several ways in which you can attach the remaining cones
to the wreath. You can wire them on individually or in groups. The fastest
method I have found and one that also produces a sturdy, weatherproof
wreath, is the hot glue method. Another method of finishing your wreath is to
apply the "rounding out" cones and the exotic ones with water-soluble linoleum paste. This paste must be applied thickly (about a teaspoonful per cone)
and it takes twenty-four hours to set up. For this reason, I let each row of
cones set overnight, before adding more.

4. Now that you have prepared your wreath base and chosen your
method of attaching the rest of the cones, you can begin rounding out the
wreath to give it more dimension. Line up all your round, more common
cones, such as loblolly, scotch pine, or pitch pine, so you can see their various
sizes. Use hot glue to attach the largest cone to the white pine base at the
bottom of the wreath. Add the next two largest cones to either side of that
one.

5. Next, take the three smallest of your round cones and attach them to
the top of the wreath. Continue adding the remainder of the cones, gluing the
largest up from the bottom and the smallest down from the top, until you
have encircled the entire wreath with a row of round cones.

6. If you are wiring or using hot glue, you may now add another circle
of round cones beside the row just attached. If you are using linoleum paste,

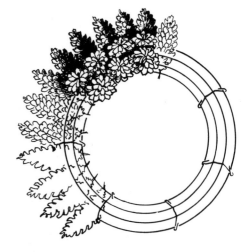

*How to apply pine cone base to a
wire-box ring. A pine cone wreath
constructed on a sturdy foundation,
such as this one, will last for many years.
For a neat, well-rounded appearance,
make sure the tips of the cones extend
the same distance beyond the outside
rim of the wire frame. The stem end of
the cones will be concealed by other
layers of cones so does not require
uniformity.*

set your project aside to dry overnight and then add your second row.

7. Once you have rounded out your wreath with the two rows of round cones, it is time to consider where you will place your most unusual, exotic pods and cones. This is easy to do because you can simply place them on the wreath (without glue), moving them around until you find the spot where they look best, and then glue them there. In order to avoid getting too many large ones on one side of the wreath, glue a certain pod on the left side, then glue one of a like kind and size on the right side. Glue the largest of the exotics to the very bottom of the wreath. Tuck small cones of hemlock, red spruce, larch, and eucalyptus pods into any cracks or spaces between the other cones.

8. My wreath has a nesting quail hiding among some delicate rhododendron pods. The three gilded round shapes near the bottom of the wreath are dried fruits from the Ginko tree, sprayed gold. Add those if you'd like.

9. Coat your masterpiece with a clear acrylic spray to bring out the many wood tones of the cones and make the wreath easier to dust. To refresh the wreath, spray it many times over the years.

One of the nice things about this wreath is that it will last practically forever. Another nice thing about it is that it is an original — no two ever look alike.

By removing the quail, this wreath may be used to encircle a punch bowl during the holidays, and it looks especially pretty with pieces of holly or other evergreens tucked among the cones.

WINTER

Winter has come and the world of Nature is at rest. The frenzy of spring, summer, and fall, of trying to capture and preserve flowers for out-of-season enjoyment, has subsided. I think of winter as a cozy time when such activities as curling up by the fireplace with a book, catching up on correspondence with friends, and perusing the seed catalogs which begin to arrive at this time are pure delights.

As you may have guessed, some of my happiest winter hours are spent in working with the flowers and other materials preserved during the growing seasons. Now that the heat is on in the house and the humidity can be controlled, I am able to work with the more fragile of these flowers. Suddenly my studio comes alive with the blooms of daffodils, roses, peonies, delphinium, and the many other jewels preserved so carefully. They can now be arranged under glass domes, in lucite boxes, in antique frames, and interesting jars, where, if you live in a humid coastal area (such as New Jersey), they will be safe from dampness and can be enjoyed for many years. Can you think of a lovelier Christmas or Hanukkah gift to present to your friends? Because you have collected and preserved the materials used to create these unique gifts, they will express your thoughtfulness as nothing else can. I also make arrangements in open baskets, silver bowls, attractive vases, and other containers that fit well with the decor of my home. I know that as soon as the spring humidity arrives, I may lose a few of the more delicate flowers to the dampness, and by midsummer these open arrangements will begin to show signs of needing attention. But nothing can equal the beauty of bouquets of roses, daffodils, marigolds, and zinnias in the dead of winter. When you consider the short life of a fresh bouquet in a heated room, you will realize how close to a miracle dried bouquets are. They will last all winter and well into spring and summer, bringing brightness and color into every room of the house. When constructing these open arrangements, I am careful to spray each flower with a clear, acrylic sealer. The sealer prevents moisture from reentering the petals. Due to the varied texture and number of flower petals, the spray may miss some areas, and this is where the humidity may seep in, causing a loss of shape or color. If you will watch for a clear, dry day in winter and take your open arrangements outdoors and respray them, you will not only freshen them, but the added sealer will lengthen the life of the arrangement.

In the color section of this book are many photographs of flowers I have dried and arranged in various types of containers. Perhaps they will give you ideas as to good color combinations, pleasing shapes of arrangements that will look well in your home, and types of interesting containers. If you have been drying flowers and storing them for winter bouquets, now is the time to put them all together and enjoy seeing a summer garden blossom in your home.

The winter months are good ones for hiking on mild days. If you take a pair of pruning shears with you and a plastic sack, you may come across all sorts of pine cone treasures, pieces of driftwood, or unusually shaped branches. Crape myrtle, rose of sharon, and yucca pods usually cling tenaciously to their branches all winter long. Clip them and take them home to add to your collection.

Forcing branches to open prematurely is another winter activity that can bring springtime right into your living room. As the winter days edge toward spring, I become eager to rush my favorite season by forcing branches of spring flowers to blossom early. Forsythia and Japanese quince are my favorites. Their yellow and pink blossoms soon have the house looking like a stage setting from *Madame Butterfly*. In order to force branches, choose those at least ¼-inch thick containing many swelling buds. The branches should be trimmed from the trees or bushes on a mild winter day, about four or five weeks before their normal blooming time. I find branches about 2 feet long to be the easiest to work with. However, if you are planning to make a floor arrangement, you may wish to cut some branches 3 to 4 feet in length. For a spectacular preview of spring in your home, try forcing apple, birch, cherry, dogwood, filbert, forsythia, maple, oak, peach, pear, pussy willow, Japanese quince, redbud, sekko willow, spicebush, or spirea. With a small hammer, crush 2 or 3 inches at the base of each branch. This will help them absorb the water more easily. Then submerge the smaller branches in the kitchen sink in warm water (about the temperature of a baby's bottle) for 2½ to 3 hours. If you are planning to make a floor arrangement with very tall branches, you will have to submerge these branches in warm water in the bathtub for 3 to 4 hours.

When the branches have soaked sufficiently, place them in deep containers of warm water. The water will need changing once a week, at which time you will have to trim the stems and crush them a bit more. You will want to check every few days to make sure the water has not evaporated, in which case add more. I find that spraying the buds with warm water several times a week (and every day when possible) helps to speed the process. This has the effect of a warm, spring rain on the buds. Until the branches begin to bloom, they should be kept out of direct sunlight, but in a location where they will receive daylight. Since the buds seem to open best in a temperature between 68° and 70°F., if your home is warmer than this, you may wish to start the branches in a cooler spot, such as basement or breezeway.

Pomegranate Wall Display

A wall arrangement is an eye-catcher, similar to a hanging basket but refreshingly different too. Use it as a Christmas decoration by making one similar to mine, an after-the-holidays design in wintery whites and blues, or as a fall accent piece in autumn colors. You could also make an attractive spring arrangement on the tray, spraying it a sunny yellow or moss green and using pastel colors in the design.

This tray-type design may also be used on a door, in place of a fall, Christmas, or spring welcome wreath.

Materials

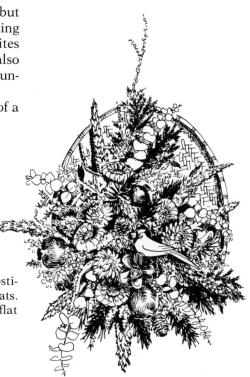

an oval woven straw tray, 17-inch

floral form

5 bare branches, any shrub

arborvitae *(Thuja)*

German statice

5 protea pods

7 stems of red uniola (any red stem or similar shape may be substituted, such as Japanese bamboo, rattail millet, broom corn, wild oats. You might also spray material which you have collected, with a flat red paint.)

5 pieces of eucalyptus

5 medium pine cones, any variety

3 white helichrysum

3 milkweed pods

1 cut cone flower with strictum center

7 strictum rosettes, smaller than the pine cones

3 dried pomegranates

1 stem of milo berries

silver spray paint

fresh holly

cardinal ornament

hot glue and glue gun, or thick white craft glue

stem wire

wire cutters

Tray-type wall or door designs are a delight to make because they go together with speed, use little material, and are quite versatile, season-wise. They add a dramatic home-decor motif wherever they are displayed.

Instructions

1. Glue a 4-inch-square block of floral foam to the tray. Mine was attached 4 inches up from the bottom and 4 inches in from the left side. This gives you the base for an offset arrangement.

2. Attach a stem wire hanger to the back of the tray.

3. While creating the design, it's a good idea to hang the tray at eye level, on a cup hook screwed into the wall, for better perception of the design.

4. Attach the foam to the tray with hot glue. You are now ready to proceed with your project. (If you used thick white glue, you may have to wait until the glue is thoroughly dry before proceeding.)

5. Spray the bare branches white and allow to dry. Insert one tall stem into the foam, so that it will extend upward about 5 inches above the top of the tray.

6. Insert the remaining white branches into the foam, flat against the edge of the tray, extending slightly over side edges and bottom rim.

7. Branches of arborvitae, air dried flat on a screen, may be added between the five white branches for a background. They should lie flat against the tray.

8. Cover the foam with German statice, using pieces about 5-inches in length. Some of these pieces should extend outward beginning to form your rounded bed of filler.

9. Insert the five protea pods now, one near the top of the tray and the others slanting outward, down the sides of the design. Refer to the illustration as you work.

10. Add the red uniola (or other spike-type material) next. Follow illustration for angles.

11. Add nine more stems of German statice, each about 5 inches in length, to the arrangement, for body and to fill it in more.

12. Add eucalyptus branches next. Follow illustration.

13. Using your selected glue, add the medium-size pine cones, attaching them to the filler.

14. Insert three white helichrysum in a triangular pattern.

15. Glue the milkweed pods to the filler at this point, also in a triangular pattern.

16. Bend the wire legs of the cardinal sideways so they will insert easily into the foam.

17. Below the cardinal glue the cut cone flower to the background filler. Glue a smaller cone in the center, if you wish.

18. Glue strictum rosettes to the filler around the edges of the arrangement, where they will show. Make sure they are not hidden in the filler.

19. Stem and insert the three pomegranates in place, triangularly. Because the pomegranates are the heaviest material in the design, rather than wire for stems, I used woody yarrow stems.

20. To add the pretty sparkle to your composition, spray a stem of milo (sorghum) with silver paint. When the paint is dry, separate the tiny clusters of berries from the stem and glue them into the design, wherever they look the prettiest.

21. Tuck a few sprigs of fresh holly or other evergreen around the bird for a finishing touch. The greens will dry in the arrangement. When they need renewing, lift them out gently, and tuck more in place.

If you want to use these instructions to make a fall design, you might wish to spray the milo gold instead of silver. If you cannot locate milo, canella berries, sweet gum balls, or hemlock cones, sprayed silver or gilded, are good substitutes.

Baby's Breath Christmas Wreath

If you have never made your own Christmas wreath, why not involve the whole family and make one this year? Wreath-making can be lots of fun, and so are fall picnic outings to find pine cones, nuts, berries, and other natural decorations.

This wreath is made on a flat, wire ring base, easily obtained from a craft or garden shop.

Materials

1 flat, wire wreath ring, 14-inch
1 roll wreath wrapping wire
white pine cones (long, soft cones with white tips)
magnolia leaves, glycerinized
assortment of decorative cones, nuts, pods, berries
assortment of red and green dried flowers
baby's breath
velvet bow, red
newspaper
wire cutters
scissors
wooden floral picks
hot glue and glue gun, white craft glue, or linoleum paste

A plain pine cone wreath can become a breathtaking creation by just the addition of a magnolia leaf halo and a "blizzard" of baby's breath all over the cones. Red and green flowers can be glued to the wreath in little groupings as shown in the illustration, and a rich red velvet bow will make it all look holiday perfect!

Instructions

1. Cover work area with newspaper.

2. Attach end of wrapping wire to top of wreath frame, wrapping it around one of the support struts several times. (See figure.)

3. When the wrapping wire is firmly attached to the wire wreath base, form a hanger loop at the top and twist the wire around the top strut several more times. (See figure.) *Do not cut wire from roll.*

4. Place three white pine cones together on wreath frame, near hanger, and wrap wire *tightly*, over and around them three times, pulling tightly. The three cones should be side by side and flat. *Do not cut the wire.* (See figure.)

5. Place the next three white pine cones halfway over the first three. The tips of these three cones will not be flat and their stem ends will be resting on the ring base. (See figure.)

6. Now wrap the wire over these three cones at their middle, repeating three times and pulling the wire taut each time.

7. Circle the entire wreath ring with sets of three cones that you wrap across the *middle* with the wrapping wire. If you wrap the cones too near the stem ends, they will not lie against the other cones properly. If you wrap them with wire too near the tip end, the wire will show, detracting from the finished wreath.

8. When your wreath ring is covered with firmly wired pine cones, wrap the wire around a support strut four or five times before cutting the wire from the roll.

The illustration shows how to attach the wrap wire to the wire wreath ring, forming a sturdy loop.

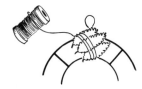

This illustration shows how to attach white pine cones to the wreath base without cutting the wire.

This illustration depicts arranging white pine cones on the wreath base in sets of three, overlapping each set halfway over the previous set.

9. At this stage, you should have a very attractive pine cone wreath that *can be used just as it is,* or you may continue the project and decorate it.

10. Place a circle of glycerinized magnolia leaves around your pine cone wreath, so you can line them up according to size and shape before attaching them.

11. Wire a wooden pick to each leaf, dip pick in glue, and glue each pick to the back of the pine cone wreath. Using the hot glue gun, you will be able to continue your project immediately. If you are using thick white craft glue or linoleum paste, you must let the glue dry before continuing.

12. Glue little clusters of decorative cones to the wreath and surround them with Christmas green, laguros (hares tails), and bright red starflowers. Any assortment of red and green flowers will do.

13. The last step is to create the frosty "blizzard" of white baby's breath before adding the red velvet ribbon bow. Tack the two streamers of the bow in place with glue to form the pretty ripple effect.

This wreath will last for many years and can be displayed indoors or out.

For an attractive holiday ring to encircle your punch bowl, you could use the plain pine cone ring. Spray it with a clear acrylic sealer and decorate it with fruit and nuts. When placed around the punch bowl, then tuck little sprigs of holly, bayberry, or other evergreens between the fruit.

Another interesting use for the plain cone wreath is to wire it over a fresh green wreath. The greens make a pretty edging for the woody pine cones and a gold or red velvet bow is all the decoration needed.

I spray my pine cone wreaths and greens with a sealer, which intensifies the woody tones and keeps the greens fresh longer. I have used these same pine cone wreaths over fresh green ones for many years, freshening them each year with a new coating of clear, acrylic spray and sometimes adding a new, gold velvet bow.

Hanukkah Menorah

Hanukkah is a delightful time of year when the house is filled with the aroma of holiday baking, the excitement of the children anticipating their gifts, and friends dropping by bringing season's greetings and good wishes. I have designed this Hanukkah menorah as a special front door decoration for the holidays or for use indoors as an attractive wall arrangement. It is an easy project to construct and one the children can enjoy helping you create.

Materials

1 sheet of heavy corrugated cardboard or lightweight plywood, 18 by 5 inches

40 white pine cones or Norway pine cones

9 stalks of mullein, pods of evening primrose, or any other tall, woody pod

15 (or so) round, rosette-type pine cones

assortment of hemlock cones, globe amaranths, beechnut pods, crape myrtle pods, hazelnuts, small white helichrysums, or other natural pods

1 can spray sealer to use on cardboard, if you are using same

1 can gold spray paint

1 can white enamel spray paint

2 pieces strong wire, 6-inch

wire cutters

stem wire

hot glue and glue gun, thick white craft glue, or linoleum paste

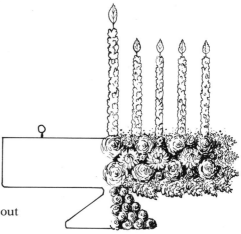

Instructions

1. Using heavy corrugated cardboard or lightweight plywood, cut out the shape of the 9-inch Hanukkah menorah. (See sketch for outline.)

2. If using cardboard, coat it with a sealer, back and front, to keep it from warping.

3. Add two wire hangers, one on each side at the top, so the finished design will hang straight.

4. Using long white pine cones or Norway pine cones, outline the base of the menorah by gluing the cones around and over the edge. (See sketch.)

5. Spray paint nine stalks of mullein with a clear sealer. (These will serve as the candles.) When the sealer is dry (it will only take a few minutes), spray them again with white enamel. Two light coats are better than one heavy coat.

6. When the white paint has dried throughly, overspray each "candle" lightly with gold spray paint to give just a hint of gilding.

7. Line up your assorted round pine cones according to size in a "cut down" corrugated carton (such as an empty soda case).

8. Spray the round cones with gold paint with several light sprayings. The corrugated box will hold them in place while you are gilding them.

9. When the cones are dry, glue them onto the menorah base with the rosette of the cone facing frontward. Hot glue makes the project go faster, but thick white craft glue or linoleum paste will also work well.

10. Using your assortment of hemlock cones or other natural dried materials, fill-in between the round pine cones. Also, fill-in the short pedestal base of the design.

11. To complete this attractive holiday door or wall decoration, glue the tallest mullein candle into the center of the menorah base. Glue four more of the mullein candles on each side of the central one. The eight shorter candles are to be the same height and the central candle higher. (Refer to the sketch.) I sometimes find it necessary to glue a popsicle stick to the back of the mullein and corrugated backing of the menorah for added support of the candles.

Because your lovely Hanukkah menorah is made of natural, sturdy materials, it can be wrapped in tissue and carefully stored away for use next year. And, for those friends who admired your handiwork, why not make several more menorahs for their homes?

This Hanukkah menorah is so beautiful when completed that you may have to make several more for friends. Any assortment of cones can be used. Once they are sprayed gold only their texture will be apparent, forming this rich-looking menorah.

An arrangement of this type is rather tailored looking and thus would be most appropriate as a gift for a favorite man in your life. It would look striking in an office, library, or den, and, although the predominating colors are red and green, with a touch gilded elegance, the design could be used throughout the winter season. The basket is a Mexican woven box. I have attached the lid to the lower part of the container with hot glue and have positioned it off center.

Holiday swags look simply elegant displayed on either side of a fireplace, on a front door, in a hallway or foyer, or on a narrow wall. Following the step-by-step instructions, you can't go wrong.

Gucci Ribbons Christmas Arrangement

It is usually difficult to choose a flower arrangement for a man. Most floral designs seem feminine in color, design, or both. Yet men certainly enjoy beautiful flowers as much as women do.

With this in mind, I designed the Gucci Christmas arrangement along tailored lines, using the ribbon that has become the hallmark of the famous Italian designer, Emilio Gucci.

I attached the two baskets in a staggered manner, using hot glue, and then sprayed them in metallic gold for richness. I glued the ribbon around the top edge of each basket with a thick white craft glue and added a separately made bow-tie.

The lower basket was stuffed with newspaper, almost to the top. Three large pine cones were then glued to the paper with thick white craft glue. To finish the lower basket I glued tiny hemlock cones between the larger cones, totally covering the newspaper. In keeping with the Christmas color scheme, I then added red lacquered berries and gilded Yakima berries.

The upper basket consists of moss-covered floral foam Christmas-green gypsy broom, and white German statice for fillers; woody pine cones tie in with the lower composition; and there are brown crape myrtle pod clusters, red roses and carnations, red Yakima berries, and gilded spore cases of the sensitive fern.

The arrangement could be used in a den or office throughout the winter season.

Holiday Swag

Wall swags of this kind look exceptionally pretty when hung on a front door, on a wall in a family room, or in pairs at either side of a fireplace chimney. You may use any variety of cones and pods; the greater the variety, the more interesting will be your swag.

My design starts out with a red velvet bow wired to the hanger. The swag is built on a heavy wire coat hanger. The hanger hook is at the top and the rest of the wire is straightened out, forming a support rod on which to build the swag.

A beautiful red dried pomegrante is at the top of my design. Three brown-tipped mahogany pods are next. From there, a variety of pods seem to tumble down the length of the swag, including a cotton pod, several curled okra pods, canella berries, purple hakea pods, protea, cut-cone flowers, tiny eucalyptus clusters, hemlock and red spruce cones, strictum, and Norway pine cones.

Each of the large cones is wired with a 12-inch-long stem wire. Individually, the cones were wired to the main support rod, and the stem wire was wrapped around the rod several times. I then coated the wrapped wire with hot glue to seal it in place. White thick craft glue would work well, but you would need to allow drying time periodically. Duco cement would be good for coating wire and would also be faster drying.

I used the Norway pine cones to outline the swag, and the

smaller cones and pods were glued to the large design as finishing touches and to fill in any gaps.

I sprayed several coats of clear, acrylic sealer on the finished design to bring out the many different wood tones. Be sure to protect the velvet bow with plastic food wrap when spraying with sealer.

Holiday Sleigh Decoration

Sleigh-shaped containers are everywhere during the holiday season, but they are just as appropriate to use throughout the winter when filled with fresh greenery and an angel. I found a little irresistible angel in a Christmas tree ornament shop, but you can use any ornament you like.

The filler I have used in this sleigh is white German statice and Christmas Green gypsy broom. I used dried ruscus in red, green, and gold to outline the arrangement, and I tucked fresh holly among the dried materials. (It can be easily replaced when no longer fresh.) The fluffed, red gingham bow fills up a lot of space (saving on filler) and adds a festive touch that is not just for Christmas.

When you discover how fast and easy this project is, you will want to make several for gifts.

A holiday sleigh can be used throughout the winter months. The little angel riding in this sleigh of greenery is a tree ornament. Fresh greens may be tucked into the arrangement and replaced when necessary.

Materials

    sleigh container
    small block of floral foam to fit sleigh
    angel ornament (or other figure)
    moss
    dried ruscus, red, green, and gold
    Christmas green gypsy broom
    white German statice
    gingham ribbon, red
    fresh holly or other evergreens (optional)
    spray paint, gold (or other color)
    thick white craft glue
    stem wire
    wire cutters
    acrylic spray, clear

Instructions

1. If you wish to change the color of the container by spraying it gold or any other color, now is the time to do it. I sprayed my sleigh a bright gold, and I also gilded several pieces of ruscus.

2. When the paint is dry, glue floral foam to inside of sleigh. Glue angel or other decoration to the foam at the center.

3. Using stem wire bent into hairpin shapes, pin the moss to cover the foam.

4. Around outer edges of sleigh, insert 5-inch stems of red or green ruscus into foam, allowing it to extend about 3 inches out of the sleigh, as a border.

"Miss Noel" looks happy and warm in her winter wonderland of dried red, white, and green natural materials. This basket design makes a truly different wall hanging for the holidays or winter months. It can also delight children visiting your home if it is hung at their eye level on the door.

5. Fill in the arrangement with green broom and highlight it with sprigs of German statice, as suggestions of snow.

6. Make a fluffy bow. Wrap wire around the center and insert the wire into the foam at the front of the sleigh.

7. Near the angel and circling her, insert the gilded ruscus.

8. Your arrangement should look quite complete without the added sparkle of holly. If you live in an area where holly thrives, you may wish to add some to your arrangement periodically. If not, silk holly is now available where you purchase silk flowers and looks amazingly realistic.

The materials used in this arrangement are very sturdy. You should be able to enjoy your holiday sleigh for many years.

Victorian Winter Display

This cheery little miss with her old-fashioned muff is standing in a field of dried ruscus, ferns, white gypsy, and German statice. Any scraps of dried material that can be used to create a woodsy scene will do for this gay holiday wall arrangement.

I discovered the doll in a Christmas shop in Myrtle Beach, South Carolina, but any interesting figurine (perhaps deer or Santa or elves) will do as well. The doll is dressed in a red velvet Victorian outfit, and so, I have incorporated red ruscus into the design. The white statice and gypsy add a frosty touch to the winter scene. I simply dipped all dried materials in thick white craft glue and glued them in place.

The basket is a 12-inch-diameter bread basket, and I have attached a wire hanger to the back rim where it won't show. A red velvet bow and fresh holly sprigs complete the festive appearance of this wall hanging or front door decoration.

This exquisite red-and-white velvety Christmas tree, frosted with blinking white tree lights, can be the highlight of your holiday buffet. Guests will find it hard to believe that you created this tree of all natural materials.

Celosia Christmas Tree

This exquisite red and white velvety Christmas tree is quite an unusual holiday accent piece. The twinkling white lights bring out the green moss background and highlight the softness of red celosia and snowy white immortelles.

Not only is this tabletop tree easier to construct than you might think, but it is long lasting and can be covered with a plastic dry-cleaning bag for storage between seasons.

I have used it as decoration for an early holiday buffet dinner and loaned it to friends for entertaining during the yuletide season.

If you did not grow celosia in your garden this summer, include it in your list of seeds for next season. The crested flowers resemble a rooster's comb, and thus, this old-fashioned plant is also known as cockscomb. (For more information on growing and drying celosia, refer to Facts About Flowers.)

Materials

rattan mat or other base, 12-inch
2 bricks of floral foam
1 string of white twinkling Christmas lights
moss
tiny, gilt angel ornament
several large heads of dried celosia
white immortelles or sweet everlasting
assorted cut pine cone flowers, deodar, or strictum rosettes
5 wooden picks
stem wire
wire cutters
hot glue and glue gun or thick white craft glue

Instructions

1. Glue one brick of floral foam, small end, to rattan mat or other base.

2. Place second brick of foam on top of first one and insert wooden picks at an angle to join both together. (See figure.)

3. Make about 50 pins by bending 4-inch-long pieces of stem wire into hairpin shape.

4. Starting at the top of the foam, pin the lights in a spiraling fashion, down the foam, being sure to end with the plug at the base. Insert pins at a downward angle to resist pulling out.

5. Next, pin moss to cover the foam and wires of the lights, being careful not to cover any of the lights.

6. Insert the wire stem of the angel into the top of the tree. If the angel has no wire, glue it in place.

7. Press the foam at the top of the tree together to make it as pointed as you would like it to be.

8. Working downward from the top, glue pieces of celosia to the moss to make a good overall pattern of red velvety celosia. It would be a good idea to separate celosia into small, medium, and large pieces. The smaller ones should go at the top of the tree, then the quarter-to-half-dollar size, and the larger pieces at the bottom.

9. In between the red celosia, glue small bunches of white immortelle or sweet everlasting also in an overall pattern.

10. Lastly, glue cut-cone flowers to the tree, placing the largest near the bottom and the smaller ones toward the top.

As you are working on your tree, stand back often to get a better perspective of the shape that is developing. You want it to be cone-shaped (triangular) when it is completed. If it needs a little filling out, simply add a suitably sized piece of celosia where needed, or a larger bunch of immortelles.

You will receive many compliments on your tree this year and you will enjoy it even more next year, because it will be ready to display by simply unpacking it.

The base of this unusual Christmas tree is two blocks of floral foam, glued together and pegged as shown here. The wooden picks give additional support to the foam. The top of the foam can either be cut to shape or pressed together to form the desired tree top shape.

What could be more charming than the Swedish custom of ushering in the spring with their arrangement of birch branches gaily decorated with colored feathers. The housewife plans it so the branches are covered with tender, new leaves by Good Friday, called "Long Friday" in Sweden.

Swedish Easter Arrangement

The Swedes have a charming custom of hastening spring's arrival. They cut or purchase branches of the silver birch tree. To the tips of these branches they bind fluffy, gaily colored chicken feathers. The branches are placed into vases of water to decorate the living room. As the spring sunshine and central heating work their magic on the buds, the branches burgeon into an array of tender green leaves among the pretty feathers. This custom is part of their preparation for Easter, so the branches are gathered in time to be covered with the little leaves by Good Friday.

As an unusual winter project, perhaps you and your children would like to make some Swedish Easter sprigs this year. If you do not live near a friendly hen house, you will be able to purchase packets of feathers from a craft and hobby shop. Because the feathers have a protective oily coating, you will need to use very hot water, tinted with food coloring, to which a teaspoon of glycerin has been added (per quart of food-coloring–water solution). The glycerin will act as a wetting agent to permit the feathers to absorb the coloring. After coloring the feathers, place them on absorbent paper to dry, and then fluff them with your fingers. Use thin wire to attach the feathers to the branches, so you will be able to remove them and save them for use again next year.

Sparkling Centerpiece

Another exciting winter project resembles an ice storm. Remember the last time you awoke to find the world encased in ice? The branches all wore crystal sleeves and icicles hung from the rooftops? The last ice storm we had turned our 12-foot holly tree into a priceless crystal ornament complete with red glass holly berries. The ice storm, though treacherous for driving, is truly one of nature's most spectacular shows.

From the safety of your kitchen, you can create some ice-crystal-encrusted dried materials from which to make a sparkling winter centerpiece. To begin, you will need to gather some woody-type weeds from the fields and meadows. They need not be perfect or even pretty, just strong and woody. Teasel and globe thistles are good for holding the crystals, and peppergrass and pennycress are strong enough to hold the "ice" and add a feathery touch to an arrangement. Corncockles, evening primrose stems, curled dock, bottle-brush pod, wheat, and tansy will also "ice" nicely.

Materials

assortment of any dry, woody-type weeds that are sturdy
metal bucket, ½ gallon
alum, one pound, in lump form
long-handled wooden spoon
soup bowl
clip-type clothespins
waxed-paper-covered tray

An easy, yet spectacular, centerpiece can be created simply by stacking silver tree balls and fresh greenery in a long tray and inserting crystallized branches to reflect the candlelight in the silver balls. Tiny red star flowers or red berries, to match the red candles, will complete your holiday design.

Instructions

1. Place an assortment of woody-type dried materials in the kitchen within easy reach of the kitchen sink.

2. Pour 1½ quarts of warm water into the metal bucket. Add one pound of lump-type alum to the water, which will become milky.

3. Place the metal bucket of alum solution on the kitchen range and turn the heat to medium. Stir constantly until the alum dissolves and the water becomes clear. This will occur *before* the solution reaches boiling.

4. When the water clears, remove the bucket from the range and place it in the kitchen sink.

5. Bring your assortment of dried materials to the sink and submerge them in the alum solution. Because they are dry, they may float, making it necessary to weight them down with a soup bowl. If the stems are long enough, clip them to the side of the bucket with the clothespins.

6. Set the bucket aside for four hours. As the solution cools, crystals will form on the dried material. Test after four hours to see if the material is covered with these icelike crystals. If not, let the bucket remain undisturbed for another hour or two.

7. Once the dried materials are covered with cyrstals, remove them from the solution and let them drain before placing them on the waxed-paper-covered tray to dry. Save all the drippings and return as much as possible to the bucket.

8. You can reuse the remaining alum solution, and, although it may be brown and ugly, reheating and stirring it will clear it up again.

9. When the solution has cleared, add more woody, dried materials and repeat Steps 5, 6, and 7.

10. The crystallized material should dry for at least twenty-four hours undisturbed, at which time it will be ready for use in a spectacular winter arrangement.

Fantasy in Ice Display

The most appropriate container for an ice crystal arrangement is a silver-colored or mirror-encased one that has a broad base. The icy branches will be heavy and could cause a narrow-based vase to tip over.

You will be amazed at how realistic your Fantasy in Ice arrangement will be. If you place it in the sun, you will be able to see every color of the rainbow in the crystals.

Materials

paraffin
silver-colored container
floral foam, shaped to extend 2 inches above rim of the container
moss
crystallized branches
3 teasel burrs, crystallized
newspaper
hot glue and glue gun, linoleum paste, or thick white craft glue
stem wire
wire cutters

Instructions

1. Protect work area with newspaper. Melt one block of paraffin in a tin can seated *in a pan of water* on the range. *Do not* place tin of wax directly on the heating surface. (See Uses of Paraffin.)

2. When the melted wax resembles clear water, pour about ½ cup into your silver-colored container.

3. Place the shaped block of floral foam into the wax in the container. Press down slightly on the foam until the wax cools, anchoring it securely to the container. This should take about five minutes.

4. Now add more melted wax to add weight, filling the container to within ½ inch of the rim.

5. Using stem wire, make hairpin-shaped pins, and pin tufts of moss onto the foam to conceal it. Also, if wax shows around the edges, tuck pieces of moss over it, so it will not show through your design.

6. Decide which of your crystallized material are the most encrusted with the sparkling ice. Save these for the front of the arrangement where they will show to the best advantage.

7. Choose branches that either are not especially attractive in shape or did not crystallize and seem more snowy than icy. Construct the main outline of your arrangement with these.

8. Establish the height of your arrangement and use hot glue, linoleum paste, or thick white craft glue on the ends of the stems before inserting them into the foam for added strength.

9. This arrangement tends to be somewhat top-heavy, so an evenly balanced design, weight-wise, seems to work best. This can be accomplished by placing a tall, lightweight stem toward the back, at the center, and then working downward on each side of that stem, forming a triangle. The heavier pieces will be used at the lower center, where the most weight should be.

10. Insert the three teasel burrs in a triangle, gluing them into the foam, and then glue all the remaining stems into the arrangement. (Refer often to the illustration while creating your design.)

Your completed arrangement will be most effective if displayed *on* a mirror. When the sun shines on it, you will be able to see every color of the rainbow flashing through the icy crystals.

Another effective way of using crystallized materials for an attractive centerpiece is to place them in a long, low, shallow container. Add several silver Christmas tree balls under and around them for reflection, and place a silver or pewter candlestick at each end of the arrangement. The flickering candlelight will reflect in the crystals and silver balls and look simply elegant. No one will ever suspect how effortless it was to construct. You will be able to pack the branches away, between sheets of tissue, in a box, until the next time you do some winter entertaining or host a silver anniversary party.

Holiday Wall Plaques

Wooden plaques are ideal for dried, natural material designs. The warmth of wood seems to tie it all together. Boards in all sizes and shapes may be purchased from your craft and hobby store. Some are

A holiday door decoration or wall plaque or gift, this design goes together easily. The board is finished in a barn-red acrylic. The glycerinized magnolia leaves were glued in place with thick, white craft glue before the assortment of cones and pods was added. The center focal point is a lotus pod. The long curvy pods are okra. Magnolia pods, deodar, teasel, eucalyptus, strictum, and white pine cones complete the design.

prefinished, and others require staining or painting. Once your board has been prepared by just a light sanding with finishing sandpaper, you are ready to give the board the finish you desire and then apply your design. Hot glue or thick white craft glue are ideal for plaque projects.

The wreath plaque shown in the illustration was made by gluing hemlock cones in a circle, tucking in small pieces of green moss and green-dyed yarrow, and adding bayberries in groups of three with glue. The project was completed by gluing tiny red flowers and a red velvet bow at a jaunty angle.

The hemlock cone basket plaque was chosen by the Society of Craft Designers for their first crafts calendar, produced in 1981.

The large holiday door decoration or wall plaque somewhat resembles a rich wood carving. Directions for it follow.

Materials

    1 plaque board, 15-inch (obtainable at craft stores)

    1 small jar of acrylic paint (barn-red, loden green, or mustard gold work well)

    9 glycerinized magnolia leaves (leatherleaf viburnum will substitute well)

    1 old, round pine cone

    1 lotus pod (or a cut-cone flower)

    3 teasel burrs

    3 okra pods (or other elongated pods)

    3 magnolia pods

    3 small white pine cones, with white tips

    5 deodar (or other rosette-type cones)

    3 strictum (or red spruce)

    3 eucalyptus pods

    2 heads of golden yarrow

    thick white craft glue

    sandpaper, fine grade

    sponge or paintbrush

    screw-type hanger

Instructions

1. Lightly sand the board until it feels smooth.

2. With a damp sponge or brush, paint the board with the acrylic paint.

3. Using thick white craft glue, glue the magnolia leaves in an attractive design to the board.

4. Glue the old, round pine cone to the center of the arrangement. This will be used to elevate the design but will not be a visual part of the design. If you would like to make your thick glue even thicker for working with the cones, simply freeze it overnight.

This wreath plaque was made by gluing a circle of hemlock cones, tucking small pieces of green moss between the cones, and then gluing bayberries, tiny red star flowers, and a red velvet bow in place. You may substitute any assortment of red and green flowers. For a fall wreath use gold and orange flowers on the brown hemlock cone wreath.

My hemlock cone basket plaque is made by gluing the hemlock cones on a suitable board to form a basket outline. Then I glue flowers to the board to look as though they have been arranged in the basket.

5. When the glue has set, attach the lotus pod to the top of the old pine cone. This will cause the lotus pod to sit high and give you room to glue teasel and other pods under the lotus to help support it.

6. Glue the 3 okra pods or other elongated pods, such as carob, catalpa, or wisteria, in a triangle as shown in the sketch.

7. Glue the magnolia pods in a triangular pattern, as well as the white pine, deodar, strictum, and eucalyptus.

8. You will now have some spaces between all of these round shapes that need filling in. Break the golden yarrow heads into small sections and glue them into all of the empty spaces.

9. Leave the board undisturbed overnight before hanging it in a place of honor. A decorative screw-type hanger will finish this beautiful design.

Red Rose Valentine

Being somewhat of a romanticist, I am fond of hearts and angels. When I found this lovely, red straw heart-shaped box in St. Thomas, I knew immediately what I would do with it. Somehow, hearts and angels and rosebuds just go together.

The lid of the box was attached to the bottom, with hot glue. A piece of floral foam was fastened into the box, also with hot glue. The angel was glued to the foam with thick white craft glue before the moss was pinned to the foam to conceal it.

Lily of the valley leaves form a delicate outline to this design. German statice and green eupatorium are the main fillers. Fluffy tufts of indian paintbrush give the illusion of a cloud surrounding the angel. Blue delphinium florets are a welcome addition to this arrangement, breaking up the reds and pinks of the roses, snapdragon florets, and the container. The yellow berries are Yakima, and the silvery leaves are dusty miller.

This design would be appropriate to give as a valentine, sweet sixteen gift, engagement gift, or simply to someone who likes hearts and angels.

The same type of arrangement can be made in a decorative box of any shape. There are many woven boxes available as well as brass, wood, and china ones.

Hearts and flowers and angels — songs have been written about them all, and now this arrangement includes them for all romanticists. The heart-shaped straw box is red and was intended for a jewelry box. This arrangement would be so very appropriate for a valentine, a birthday, an anniversary, a newborn infant, a sweetheart . . . any time you would like to send some love.

FACTS ABOUT FLOWERS

The flowers described in this chapter are those that dry well, can be easily grown in most gardens, and are not commonly seen in dried arrangements. The ajuga, bergamot, candytuft, cornflowers, crape myrtle, English daisies, and pansies are included. Some, such as carnations, celosia, hydrangea, poinsettias, and roses, are listed because they require special treatment if they are to dry to perfection. Other flowers in this section have a fascinating history that makes enjoyable reading: the crocus, goldenrod, tansy, helichrysum, roses, and tulips.

One flower in particular, the starflower, is brand new on the scene. It is not being grown commercially and is not discussed in any other book of this kind to date. The information in this chapter tells you how to grow this unusual looking plant, when to harvest it, what to do with the pods, and even how to change its color.

The Quick Reference Chart in the back of the book lists many other flowers alphabetically. The chart gives you several methods from which to choose that will preserve the flowers well, and it is arranged to give you this information at a glance.

We think of the flowers in this section as American because we have seen many of them in our gardens since childhood. However, I think you will be amazed to discover that a great many are immigrants from all over the world.

It will add a whole new dimension to a lovely arrangement when you can tell the recipient some of the interesting facts about the flowers it contains.

Ajuga *(Ajuga* species*)*

Ajuga, also known as bugleweed, is an excellent and fast-growing ground cover. It is a member of the mint family and flourishes in almost any situation. We have some growing in full sun and some hiding under the forsythia, philadelphus, and rhododendron in our garden.

The *Ajuga reptans atropurpurea* grows 6 to 12 inches high and has beautiful, dark bronze foliage. The leaves dry well in the microwave oven, without silica gel, and also process well in glycerin and water. The flowers are most often bright blue, although they also come in pink and white.

Our garden appears to have a carpet of royal blue in late spring and early summer, as the ajuga creates a rich background for the other wakening flowers. Being a perennial, it blooms all of a sudden while you've been concentrating on the annuals! This is a bonus for the flower gardener, as well as for those preserving flowers for future enjoyment.

Ajuga genevensis brockbankii flowers grow to 6 inches, have showy spikes of blue, and flower in the summer. Ordinary garden soil plus space for expansion is all they require, as they will spread by creeping.

I most often air dry these bottle-brush–shaped blooms if I am using them for body in an arrangement. Otherwise, I prefer drying them in silica gel in the microwave oven.

Ammobium *(Alatum grandiflorum)*

This delightful immigrant from Australia grows in a rather unruly manner, so you will not want to include it in your decorative flower plantings. It produces dainty but sturdy, miniature daisylike flowers that add a fresh quality to any dried arrangement. It is a perennial in warm, dry areas of the country.

Although ammobium (also known as winged everlasting) grows in yellow only (with the bracts beneath them brilliantly white, giving the appearance of a little white daisy), they are easy to dye. I frequently dye some pale pink, yellow, lavender, powder blue, and apricot with very natural results.

Broadcast the seed in a light, sandy soil, in full sun when the trees have leafed out. For drying, cut the flowers well before they have fully opened. I find air drying to be a most satisfactory method.

Bergamot *(Monarda species)*

There are several *Monarda* species, members of the mint family. Wild bergamot is lilac- to purple-colored; lemon mint is white or pinkish and lemon-scented. They are known rather interchangeably as bee-balm, Oswego tea, American Melissa, and fragrant balm. Their leaves, as well as their flower heads, are exceedingly fragrant.

This old-fashioned plant can be found in July and August from Quebec to Michigan and south to Georgia. It thrives in hot, dry areas, in ordinary or even poor soil, and is a perennial. It tends to become a bit weedy and, therefore, needs thinning out from time to time.

The petals of the flower head are unusual and dry beautifully, and are exceptionally welcome in dried bouquets. My preferred method for preserving these lovely blooms is to use preheated silica gel.

Blue Sage *(Salvia farinacea)*

In French, *sage* means "wise"; in Latin, it means "to be healthy." Dioscorides, Pliny, and Theophrastus mentioned sage in their writings so long ago, and, sage in the garden is said to prolong life.

There are some 500 members of the salvia family. The species most sought after for dried floral arrangements is *Salvia farinacea*, sometimes called "summer salvia."

The sages are grown as annuals in our garden, but many plants winter-over and pop up the second and third year. These lavender-blue, spike-type flowers on blue stems are a joy to air dry. Don't have too many in a bunch or you will lose some of the color. I frequently lay individual stems of the blue sage on screening, and it dries with excellent form and color.

Turn to Method 5 for instructions on drying blue sage rapidly in the microwave oven.

Bridal Wreath *(Spirea arguta multiflora)*

The bridal wreath growing in our garden is of the *arguta* variety. In early May it bursts into bloom, almost totally concealing the potting shed. The brides of long ago must have looked lovely wearing wreaths of this delicate flower in their hair.

The shrub grows well in ordinary soil and likes full sun. To dry the branches, simply cut them when they are fully open and hang them individually in a dark, well-ventilated room. Ours usually dry in three to five days, depending on the weather. Because it rains a great deal at "bridal wreath blooming time," be sure to pick branches when they have not been made soggy in the rain.

Candytuft *(Iberis* species*)*

A native of Spain, southern Europe, and northern Africa, candytuft will also be quite happy growing in your garden. My garden is made lacy and lovely each spring and early summer by the blooms of the perennial *Iberis semper-virens.*

Did you ever make little May baskets of wildflowers, hang them on the doorknob of friends' houses, ring the doorbell, and disappear before they could open the door to discover this first little basket, full of springtime? To add a gift of a perennial to a friend's garden is even nicer, for it will bloom to surprise your friend with springtime for many years.

There is also an annual white candytuft *(Iberis amara),* so if you are looking for the *perennial* variety, it will pay to verify that that is what you are purchasing at the nursery. Candytuft grows well in my sunny, rather dry rock garden. Some species grow to 18 inches tall, so, if you are looking for an edging plant or a rock garden delight, you'd better check the expected height.

To dry these lacy flowers, refer to the Quick Reference Chart. For snowy white results it is important to pick candytuft when dry to the touch. Leave a 2-inch stem on each bloom for easy handling later, and dry in an upright position in silica gel.

Carnations *(Dianthus* species*)*

Carnations are one of the most popular flowers for boutonnieres and prom bouquets because of their spicy scent, long-lasting qualities, and their ability to accept dyes for matching gowns. They come in many natural colors, from palest pink to salmon, and from lavender to red.

Carnations and pinks are easy to grow in well-drained, loose or sandy soil, but they do need full sun. For blooms *next year* you will have to sow the seeds this summer and let them winter-over. Plants are usually easy to find at roadside stands that sell bedding plants.

Carnations and pinks dry with excellent color and good petal separation. My preferred method is using preheated silica gel, or silica gel and the microwave oven.

Before drying the large calyx blooms, tie a piece of nylon sewing thread securely around the calyx where it meets the flower head. This procedure will hold the petals together while they are drying so the carnation will retain its natural shape when dry. I also drop household cement into the center of the carnation before drying it as an added precaution.

Refer to the Quick Reference Chart for methods and timing recommendations.

Plumed Celosia (Celosia argentea)

This type of celosia resembles silky, feathery plumes. It comes in colors from apricot brandy to forest fire scarlet. Like the crested cockscomb, plumed celosia will bloom from midsummer to frost.

To obtain the best possible color in drying this type of bloom, I suggest you cut off the entire stalk, near the soil. Remove all leaves and hang the stalk by one of its strong side shoots to dry. By this method, the individual plumes are separated while drying and retain brighter color. To bunch plumes for drying would create a damp mass of plumes with poor air circulation around the individual plumes. The result would be brown water-stained flowers.

Another effective way of drying plumed celosia with good color retention is to hang the separate plumes on the drying screen shown on page 13. If you stand a screen of this type on end, it will hold quite a few plumes. Simply insert the stems into the holes of the mesh. I also have some mesh of this type nailed between the roof supports of the attic, to which I attach S-shaped hooks of individual plumes or short sections of the stalk.

Plumed celosia is valuable as a filler in dried arrangements, sometimes adding body to an arrangement without actually becoming part of the design. When the arrangement is completed, the celosia is not visible. At other times, the colorful, feathery dried plumes add a light, soft touch to an otherwise woody fall design and, in this instance, become very much a part of the overall design.

Another place I like to use these flowers is on decorative brooms. Their bright colors can add something special, and their plume-type appearance fits in well with the broom shape.

Cockscomb (Celosia cristata)

This crested celosia is my favorite type for drying. The velvety shades of red of this old-fashioned flower truly resemble a rooster's comb.

Some varieties grow to measure a foot or more across the top, and because of their tremendous size are often overlooked for use in fresh flower arranging. When using celosia in dried flower arrangements, I break it into pieces of the size required, and, using the hot glue gun or wired picks, I stem the individual pieces of the flower head.

It intrigues me that these gigantic flowers come from seeds that are smaller than poppy seeds. If planted early, as soon as danger of frost is past, they will bloom from midsummer until frost.

The varieties Red Velvet, Floradale Crimson, and Fireglow are my favorites for drying, as they keep their vibrant shades of red. Floradale Rose-pink dries a delicate dusty rose and is lovely in colonial designs.

To dry crested celosia with excellent color retention, I use a two-part system. Pick the blooms at about noon when the sun has evaporated the morning dew. Because of their dense petal construction, water is easily trapped deep in the blooms. Place the flower stems in a bucket of water in a dark corner of the garage or similar area, for three days. During this period, the head will relax and droop, allowing moisture trapped inside to dry. Now hang each stem of celosia separately to continue drying in a warm attic. The flowers will revert to their original shape and dry true to color in about ten days, depending on the weather.

You sometimes see celosia that has been dried and is an ugly, faded brown shade. The brown comes from water stain, the result of water being trapped inside the flower head, and the flowers were hung to dry as soon as they were picked, without first allowing the moisture to escape from within the bloom.

If, while pulling the flower heads apart to use in your arrangements, you catch the little black seeds that fall from the upper stem, you will be able to plant them in your garden next spring.

The hanging placemat arrangement on page 58 is a good example of how effective crested celosia can be in a dried design.

Cornflower (Centaurea cyanus)

Bachelor's button, another popular name for the beautiful cornflower, is a favorite of mine for use in dried bouquets. I prefer the blue varieties because they dry true to color, retain their pretty shape, and are easy to air dry.

The best method I have found for air drying these delicate blooms is to clamp each stem with a bobby pin on a wire coat hanger. This separates the individual heads, preventing them from tangling, and gives plenty of room for good air circulation, which promotes rapid drying. (See figure, page 13.)

The cornflower may also be dried in silica gel, preheated silica gel, or silica gel and the microwave oven. If you have a good many to dry, I suggest using the hanger method for most and drying a few choice blooms in the preheated silica gel or microwave oven.

The cornflower is originally from southern Europe and is the national flower of Germany. It behaves like a biennial in New Jersey, but may also be planted as an annual.

When the trees leaf out, scratch or rake the seeds into ordinary garden soil. Due to the sprawling nature of this plant, I prefer to situate it at the back of the garden where it will not detract from the rest of the floral display. Some varieties grow to 30 inches, so allow for this when planting. Exceptions are the dwarf varieties that produce a neat, bush-type plant. Jubilee gem, a good, clear blue, is a dwarf, and produces a beautiful double bloom.

Cosmos (Cosmos hybrids)

These tall, delicate flowers originated in Mexico. Because of their single-petal nature, they dry rapidly in preheated silica gel. It is important to preserve the natural cup shape of the bloom and this can be done quite easily by following instructions under Method 2.

Burpee has a semi-double variety, Klondike cosmos, that is early flowering and comes in a bright fiery red, golden orange, and several other intense colors. It grows to just 2½ to 3 feet and produces a neat plant.

There are early and late varieties of this plant, so check the seed packet for this information. If you live north of Boston, I would suggest using only the early varieties.

Crape Myrtle *(Lagerstroemia indica)*

The spectacular crape myrtle is sometimes called "Indian Lilac" and actually grows wild in Australia and tropical Asia. It is the most popular and easiest shrub to grow for southern gardens and even survives as far north as the New York City area. Mine does quite well on the sunny side of the house in ordinary well-drained soil.

If you plant crape myrtle, not only will your garden become a riot of color every summer, with a profusion of crinkled crapelike flowers, but it will supply you with a source of lovely flowers to air dry by the hanging method. In the fall your garden will be covered with the intricate wooden flower pods that are so pretty in dried arrangements, as well as cone and pod projects.

Crape myrtle comes in deep rose, pale lavender, and white.

Crocus *(Crocus* species*)*

The crocus is a member of the Iris family *(Iridaceae)*. One variety, *Crocus vernus*, flowers very early in the spring, pushing the melting snow aside to herald in the new season. There is another species, the purple *Crocus sativus*, and also the blue *Crocus speciosus* that bloom in the fall. Both dry well, the latter being not so susceptible to the hazards of humidity.

If you are planting the early-flowering type of crocus for the first time, do so in the fall (August to October). The autumn-flowering kinds should be planted in July or early August. All crocus grow well in ordinary well-cultivated garden soil; leaf mold rather than animal manure should be dug into the ground when preparing for them. If the soil is at all heavy, plenty of grit should be worked in, as the bulbs flourish best in well-drained soil. The flowers do not open properly or show their full beauty if partly shaded, so be sure to choose a planting area in full sun. Avoid planting them near maple trees, which emit a gas fatal to crocus. For best results, crocus bulbs require dividing every three or four years.

Because bulb plants receive their nourishment through their leaves, it is important to protect them from the grass cutters at your house. Once the flowers have ceased blooming for the season, the leaves do begin to look a bit unkempt, but, if you are anticipating blooms next spring, protect them until they have died all the way back and turned brown before trimming them. A chicken wire screen around the bulb patches will mark the areas. For an alternate method of foliage protection, see Daffodils.

Crocus *(krokos)* is the Greek name for saffron. The fall-flowering variety, *Crocus sativus*, blooms from September into November when the rest of the garden appears rather devastated. The pistil of this grayish purple species has a reddish orange stigma, divided deeply into three parts. This is the saffron used to color rice a sunny yellow and used as a culinary flavoring.

Before bringing a crocus indoors to dry, preheat a cup of silica gel, and pour an inch of this preheated gel into a second cup. Cut the crocus stem near the base of the flower. Seat the crocus in the second cup and fill-in around and inside the bloom with the silica gel from the first cup. When the flower is completely covered with silica gel, cover the cup with plastic wrap, date it, and set aside for twelve hours. By pouring a little silica gel out of the cup, the flower tips will be exposed. Test for dryness. If they are papery dry to the touch, continue pouring silica gel out of the cup until you can safely pick up the crocus. It should be dry. Place your finger on the stem stub for a minute. If it feels cool, there may still be some moisture in the stem. In this case preheat about 2 inches of silica gel in a cup and seat the crocus stem in this for a full day to finish drying. This also should be covered with plastic wrap.

As soon as my crocus blooms are thoroughly dry, I coat the back of the petals with melted paraffin, using a small paintbrush to strengthen them. I then arrange them in a glass jar or dome, usually gluing them to bright green moss with clear silicone tub sealer. If you use an ordinary glue, the moisture from the glue will cause the crocus to wilt.

Daisy, English *(Bellis perennis)*

This is the daisy of poets. It looks more like a mini-pompon and is pictured in my arrangement in the oriental basket on page 52.

In Europe, this low-growing rock garden or edging plant is a perennial. In our garden in New Jersey, it behaves as a biennial. I grow the pink and white types because they dry with perfect color retention. The deep crimson and carmine varieties tend to darken while drying.

Plant in well-drained soil if you want them to winter-over; they cannot tolerate icy water at the roots during the spring thaw. If you live in the warmer states, you will not have to worry about this problem, and your daisies may grow for several years without having to be replaced. They do not like clay or heavy loam, so, for best results, plant in a sandy soil and in partial shade.

Preheated silica gel will dry an abundance of these blossoms in just a day. I have dried as many as fifteen in a 12-by-12-inch container.

These lovely little flowers make nice finishing touches to an arrangement and can often be glued into position without stemming.

Daffodil *(Narcissus* species*)*

The trumpet narcissus variety of daffodil is the showiest and most easily grown of the innumerable species and variations of the genus, *Narcissus*.

Planting is easy—one bulb to a hole. But because you are planting for many years of blooming, it pays to give a little thought to soil preparation. Dust the area where the bulbs are to be planted with 5 pounds of bonemeal per 100 square feet. If you have some compost, a 1-inch layer should be spread over the bonemeal. Spade the area to a depth of about 9 inches and then apply another dressing of bonemeal to the new surface and fork it in.

A common mistake is in planting bulbs too near the surface. Large bulbs must be planted in a hole allowing them 4 to 5 inches of soil covering. Medium size bulbs will do with 3 to 4 inches and the smaller bulbs with 2 to 3 inches of soil covering. After planting the bulbs, fill the holes with soil and step on them to compress the earth around the bulbs.

After blooming, it is most important that the leaves are not cut back until they have completely died back to the soil level. As recommended for the crocus leaves, chicken wire protectors can mark the daffodil beds for the grass cutter at your house.

When arranging fresh daffodils, you will have more pleasing results if you remember that daffodils and narcissus do well with very little water. For this reason they can be arranged in a shallow dish among some pretty pebbles. Once they have been dried, this is a very pretty way to arrange them *without* water.

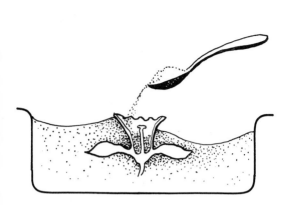

Gently cover the dafffodil with silica gel and be careful to continually brace the outside and the inside of the trumpet with silica gel as you work. This way the shape of the flower will be perfectly retained.

Refer to the Quick Reference Chart for the recommended drying time and methods. My preferred method of drying these harbingers of spring is to use preheated silica gel. You will note on the chart that the daffodils will be dry in only twelve hours. If the twelve hours are up at 2:00 A.M., I do not recommend that you jump out of bed to rescue the daffies. They will wait safely until you have had your first cup of coffee.

Use the same procedure for burying the daffodils in silica gel as you would for the crocus. While covering the bloom, be careful to support the trumpet, inside and out, with the desiccant, so that the flower will not collapse under its weight. (See figure.)

Dahlia *(Dahlia* species*)*

All of our present-day varieties of this lovely flower descend from a few wild species found in the mountains of Mexico and Guatemala. There are now more than two thousand varieties developed mostly through American hybridization, and they bloom from July until frost.

For drying purposes, I prefer the dwarf varieties, singles, and pompons. The larger, more petalled blooms have a slight stickiness that makes it difficult to remove the silica gel from the petals.

Dahlias need lots of sun and water and rich garden loam for profuse blooming. Restricting the plant to just two or three main shoots will give you the best bloom. Dahlias come under the heading of "tender perennials," which means they will not winter-over in most parts of the country. You can, however, dig the tubers after the first frost and store them (at 35° to 45° F.) for division and planting next year.

Preheated silica gel, or silica gel and the microwave oven are my favorite ways to preserve these blooms.

Dogwood *(Cornus florida)*

The most breathtaking display of dogwood in bloom I have ever seen was in Atlanta, Georgia. There actually are dogwood tours that run each hour through the blooming areas.

Forty varieties of dogwood are native to the eastern United States. In the Northeast, flowering occurs in mid-May. We have pink and white in our garden, and there is also a russet-red variety.

The scarlet fall foliage presses well on the branch, and individual leaves preserve well in a glycerin-and-water solution.

When drying the lovely flowers (bracts), silica gel should be preheated before bringing the blooms into the house, as they wilt rapidly. Hammer-crushing their stems and placing them in warm water, however, will revive the blossoms. To dry the flowers, I leave only an inch-long stem on each flower and place about six of them together in a 6-inch-diameter container. They have a very low moisture content. A cookie tin serves very well.

While they are drying, I place the branch on which they grew on top of the refrigerator to dry (or in the attic). The flowers dry quickly (see Quick Reference Chart), but the branch may take a full month. To test for dryness, try snapping it. If it breaks, it is dry; if it bends, allow more drying time. When the branch is dry, I use my hot glue gun to reattach the dogwood blooms to the branch. Three branches of this type make a simple, but truly lovely, oriental-style arrangement.

The flowers should be sprayed back and front with a matte-finish acrylic sealer, and the backs of the petals should be coated with paraffin for long-lasting enjoyment. Let sealer dry well before using the paraffin.

Geraniums *(Pelargonium zonale)*

Geraniums will give you brilliantly colored blooms to enjoy and to dry year-round, for they are just as happy on a sunny windowsill or sun porch in the winter as they were in your summer garden, terrace, or window box.

The individual florets press well and retain their beautiful colors indefinitely. I have some in a pressed frame design that was made in 1961, and the color is still vibrant.

The unusual, large Lady Washington geranium florets are each the size of a rhododendron floret and actually resemble an azalea more than they do a geranium. These florets dry to perfection in the preheated silica gel or silica gel and the microwave oven. Three of these bright coral florets were used in the Colonial Five-Finger Vase Arrangement on page 64.

By air drying them in a hot, summer attic, I have dried the bright rose-pink Showgirl variety of geranium and the Ringo Rose variety with excellent color retention and a minimum of shriveling. They must be hung singly to avoid loss of florets from tangling.

In frost-free areas, geraniums are perennials and require pinching off the shoots that may make the plant a straggler.

The original geraniums were natives of South Africa, and through hybridization, we now have more than 650 varieties.

Globe Amaranth *(Gomphrena globosa)*

This clover look-alike from India was introduced to America by George Washington, and it is still planted in the gardens at Mount Vernon. It is easy to grow and, because it is quite heat-resistant, is most often seen in gardens in the South and Midwest.

The Greek word *amarantos* means "unfading," and these charming flowers truly live up to their name. The ones I have used in the arrangements in this book were grown in 1975, and, as you can see, their colors are still jewellike.

For planting in your garden, I recommend the dwarf variety, Buddy, that only grows to 9 inches. The hybrid haageana will grow to 20 inches and the mixed colors between 18 and 24 inches. Buddy is a bright reddish purple and grows uniformly, making it a good bedding plant.

I find that soaking the seeds in water for three to four days aids germination. Spread the wet, cottony seed mass thinly over the top of the soil, in late May.

Globe amaranths air dry to perfection, keeping their brilliant colors and roundness of form. The stems will harden but may require reinforcing with wire and tape for use in arrangements. When bunching for hanging, leave about a 5-inch stem on each flower.

Quite often I use globe amaranths as finishing touches in an arrangement by simply gluing them in place once the main design is completed.

Globe Flower *(Trollius* species*)*

At first look, you might mistake these large yellow flowers as gigantic buttercups. They are native to Siberia and Scotland and so are quite hardy in the

Northeast. At night, they close into little globe shapes, from which they get their name.

In order to thrive they require planting in deep, moist soil. Beside a stream or lily pond would be ideal. I dry the individual flowers in silica gel and the microwave oven and then wire them for use in arrangements similar to the way I use the individual hydrangea florets.

Globe flowers press well and hold their color.

Goldenrod (*Solidago* species)

There are eighty species of goldenrod native to the United States. The generic name, from the Latin, signifies "to make whole" and refers to the healing properties which have been attributed to the genus.

All species will air dry well, both in their immature green stage and their golden bloom. For best results when drying the flowers, pick the stems just as the buds are opening.

Of the more than forty species to be found in the Northeast, my favorites are the sweet goldenrod (*Solidago odora*), whose aroma permeates my drying room with the scent of anise, and the strong, showy seaside goldenrod (*Solidago sempervirens*). This seaside variety has fleshy stems and so takes longer to dry, but it also has beautiful large flower heads that can be spotted along the salt marshes and rocky shores of the Atlantic coast from August to October. Last November, I was surprised to find quite a bit growing along the coast. My mother and I picked it and spread it out on the floor and seats of the car. Two days later, the goldenrod was dry and ready to use. The sun shining on the car had created enough heat to dry this super wet variety.

Goldenrod and ragweed (see figures) are difficult to tell apart by just looking at their golden flower heads (ragweed causes hay fever; goldenrod does not). For this reason, I have included a sketch of each, showing the type leaves to look for when picking goldenrod. Mixed in with the flower heads, goldenrod has tiny, sliverlike leaves. The leaves become larger as they grow down the stems toward the roots. Ragweed has leaves that have ragged edges and are large all the way up into the flower head.

Grape Hyacinth (*Muscari botryoides*)

These charming plants are in bloom with the daffodils and persevere until the last tulips are finished for the season. They dry absolutely perfectly in preheated silica gel in just twelve hours, and they keep their bright blue color for years.

The most brilliantly colored of all the grape hyacinths is *Muscari armeniacum*, which is a heavenly blue. The flower stems reach a height of 8 to 9 inches and the grapelike clusters of bright blue flowers provide glorious groups of color in the spring months. This variety also grows in white and pink.

Bulbs must be planted as early as possible in the autumn, preferably August or early September, as they start into growth far sooner than most spring-flowering bulbs. Their leaves will appear above ground in just a few weeks. With later planting, the bulbs will have little chance to become well rooted before cold weather sets in. This could cause a lessening of blooms the first year.

The bulbs should be planted 3 inches apart and covered with 2 inches of soil. They may be left undisturbed for many years until they become so

Ragweed, a main cause of hay fever, is pictured on the left. Notice how the leaves have a ragged edge. This is a good way to remember the difference between ragweed and goldenrod. One variety of goldenrod is sketched on the right. Notice the slivers of leaves in the flower heads.

crowded that they fail to bloom freely. At that time, after the leaves have completely died back and turned yellow, lift and separate the bulbs. Replant the larger bulbs and coax the small ones along for a year in a "nursery border," before planting them where you would like to display them for years.

Muscari do well in any ordinary garden soil in window boxes and spread rapidly.

Because of their strong, clear colors, they are excellent to use in pressed flower designs, as well as in flower arrangements. One of my favorite ways of displaying them is at the base of a daffodil arrangement under a glass dome. The grape hyacinths are glued to the moss-covered base of the arrangement as though they were growing there. The striking contrast between the *Muscari* and sunny yellow daffodils is quite breathtaking. Sometimes I slip a quaint, dried mushroom in between the *Muscari* for a woodsy look.

Helichrysum *(Helichrysum bracteatum)*

The helichrysum is a native of Australia and is the flower which we generally call "strawflower." They appear in the florist shops and supermarkets every September, and who can resist taking a bunch of them home?

The first thing you should do with these flowers is put them into a plastic bag and seal it with a twist-tie. Then, place the bag of strawflowers into the freezer overnight. This procedure will give your flowers many months of additional life. One of the questions which I am frequently asked is, "Why do these everlasting flowers sometimes fall apart?" The main cause is moths looking for appropriate nests in which to deposit eggs. By freezing the flowers (which does not harm them at all), you eradicate any life in those eggs and may even get several seasons of enjoyment from the same flowers.

If you grow your own helichrysums, another way of assuring longer life for the flowers and eliminating moth eggs is to put the helichrysums in the microwave oven on a paper towel, and set the timer on "high" for two minutes. *Immediately* upon removal from the oven, insert wire stems into the flower heads before they dry further. Otherwise, you will not be able to pierce the heads with the wires, as they will be too dry.

Another reason that helichrysums sometimes shatter is that they are picked past their prime. If you are growing your own flowers for drying, pick them just as they are opening. By the time they are dry, they will have opened to a perfectly formed flower shape. When commercial growers gather these flowers for mass sale, they wait until the flower is almost fully open. By the time it dries, the center (seed receptacle) is popping up, ready to scatter seeds, or else it pops up shortly after your flowers are introduced to your heated home.

If you are an apartment dweller, I recommend you grow a packet of dwarf variety, mixed colors, in your terrace or windowsill planters. They only grow to 12 inches and produce a nice compact, neat-looking plant. They will produce an abundance of medium-size flowers, provided they receive lots of sun.

For those of you who are not apartment dwellers, the other varieties of helichrysums produce plants that are not so neat, but the blooms are larger. Burpee's Bikini series, for instance, grows to 3 feet and some of the blooms are 2 inches across. The Bikinis may be had in individual colors as well as mixed. There are pink, fiery red, golden, and crimson Bikinis. If you know you will be making spring or Easter arrangements for friends, you may want to plant a packet of pink only. Admirers often mistake them for pink chrysanthemums in my spring arrangements. If you plan to work with your dried materials mostly in the fall, the mixed seeds or golden Bikinis might be best.

Helichrysums appreciate a well-enriched, light soil and make a very good showing with only occasional watering when the soil is dry.

To dry these flowers, remove their natural stems and insert a stem wire into the head of each partially opened bloom. Stand the wire stems in a coffee can so the flowers will dry in an upright position for about five days.

Hydrangea *(Hydrangea macrophylla)*

Since the primary flower heads of this shrub are usually quite large, I recommend preserving the secondary blooms, which are much smaller and appear beneath the main bloom. You might also want to dry some individual florets from the primary head in silica gel for delicate accents to your arrangements, or to press a goodly number of various sizes for use in pressed frames, lampshades, candle decoration, stationery, and so on. You will have plenty of time to gather hydrangeas, since they bloom from summer to late fall.

There are about thirty-five varieties of hydrangea, a member of the saxifrage family and native to China and Japan (where it grows to 12 feet). It may surprise you by changing its color from pink to blue. The acid in your soil is the determining factor. The deeper pink the flower is normally, the more intense will be the blue of the blooms after the use of a blueing powder sold by garden supply dealers and nurserymen for that purpose. It provides proper acidity.

To dry hydrangeas, cut a new stem (not old wood), if possible. Strip the leaves from the stem and cut the stem on a diagonal to a length sufficient to fit into a narrow olive bottle or tall glass (with head resting on the rim for support). Add about 2 inches of water to the jar and place the hydrangea stem into the water. Leave the jar in a warm place away from direct sun until all of the water has been absorbed. This method of drying prevents the top petals from shriveling as the head dries. Since the stem will still contain moisture, transfer it to a dry jar to permit thorough drying.

The entire hydrangea head can be successfully dried in silica gel. Because the results are excellent when drying the "stem-in-water" way—which I prefer for preserving full hydrangea heads—it may be done either way. But stem-in-water drying allows you to avoid having to dust the silica gel from the petals and enables you to use your silica gel to dry other flowers while the full hydrangea head is drying nicely in the jar. One of the flowers you may be drying in the silica gel would be the large, individual hydrangea florets that you will be using as single flowers. I bury the individual florets in preheated silica gel, face up, for just one day. The color will be as vibrant when the florets are dry as they were when growing. When you have removed all of the florets from the main head for pressing or drying singularly, hang the remaining head to air dry, and it will resemble a blue yarrow.

Maidenhair Fern *(Adiantum pedatum)*

Nothing will give your arrangements the softness and sparkle of a fresh flower design quicker than the addition of fern. Frequently, glycerinized dark green or brown leatherleaf fern is seen in arrangements. When commercially processed, green dye is sometimes added to the glycerin-and-water solution. If you live in an area where you can gather fern along the roadside or in the woods, you can glycerinize your own ferns by following the directions beginning on page 27 of this book.

I also press several books full of fern each year for use in dried arrangements and pressed flower projects. It is best to take the pressing books to the picking site so the ferns will not curl and wilt on the way home.

As lovely as all the glycerinized and pressed ferns are to work with, my favorite is the maidenhair fern *(Adiantum pedatum)* processed in silica gel. Magically, the fern fronds dehydrate in the silica gel but emerge as supple and fresh looking as when they were growing! They actually appear freshly picked and are neither dull nor brittle.

The name *Adiantum* means "unwet," and I am sure this has something to do with the unique results obtained when drying this lacy fern.

Because of the low moisture content of ferns, they can be dried many layers deep if you allow an inch of silica gel between layers. Your lovely ferns will be ready to use in just three days.

Mock-Orange *(Philadelphus coronarius)*

The sweet-scented mock-orange dries beautifully in preheated silica gel. I have used it in several arrangements pictured in this book.

It grows wild in southern Europe and Asia Minor and has been prominent in gardens for more than three hundred years. In our garden it blooms from May to July on bushes which are 7 feet high. From this you can see that the bushes make a lovely hedge-type planting. When the pretty blossoms are finished for the season, I use their starlike calyx in dried designs.

To dry the blooms, cut the stems about 5 inches in length and use preheated silica gel. This is my preferred method. For other methods and timing refer to the Quick Reference Chart.

Pansy *(Viola* hybrids*)*

Violas and pansies are perennials, flowering from early May through the summer. If the blooms are picked often, the plants will be discouraged from going to seed and will bloom more profusely. In severely cold climates, you may wish to plant pansies every spring, treating them as annuals.

The pretty little pansy faces seem to be made of velvet, and, as you can see in the Pansies-and-Blossoms Mirror Display on page 65, they dry exactly that way. I prefer drying pansies in silica gel in the microwave oven because the silica gel is easier to remove from the petals when they are dried in preheated silica gel.

Pansies make an attractive border for spring-flowering bulbs if planted in front of the daffodil and tulip beds. They adapt well to window boxes and apartment terrace planters too, as long as they are in a fairly rich well-drained soil and in moderate sun. They prefer cool weather. If you wish to start them from seed, plant them in your garden in midsummer and protect them with a mulch over the winter months.

In the South and Pacific southwest, seeds may be planted in the fall for spring blooms.

Peonies *(Paeonia* species*)*

Peonies are natives of China where they have been grown for more than twenty-five hundred years. These large, yet delicate, rose-scented flowers thrive in most parts of the United States. They dry so well, retaining their fresh appearance, that you will want to smell them.

I prefer drying peonies in separate containers because of their size (some reach 8 inches across). Also, because of their size, you will want to dry some partially opened blooms so that you will have several sizes of flowers to work with when you arrange them.

The tree peony blooms about two weeks earlier than the herbaceous type and dries with all its shiny satin petal finish intact.

The red peony retains its perfect red coloring unlike other flowers of this shade of red, which darken when dried.

Because of the glossy, ornamental foliage, you will want to press some of the leaves and to process some in glycerin and water.

Poinsettias *(Euphorbia pulcherrima)*

I have never seen this magnificent flower in a dried arrangement. One of the reasons is the size of each bloom. An enormous amount of silica gel would be required to cover a flower of this size, and the layers of bracts would also cause a drying problem. Another deterrent to drying a poinsettia is that this plant is a member of the milkweed family; thus both the stems and bracts contain a sticky, milky white sap. This fluid sap would not only cause the drying process to take a long time, tying up your silica gel, but it would be quite undesirable to have the sap bleeding into the desiccant.

When a friend asked me if it were possible to dry poinsettias, my answer was that they are not one of the flowers recommended for drying. But . . . the more I thought about it, the more of a challenge it became to find a way to dry this beautiful flower. The method I developed is quite rapid, requires no silica gel, and will reward you with lovely, red poinsettias to enjoy long after the plant has stopped blooming. It requires the use of a microwave oven. You will also need three oven-proof custard cups and a supply of paper napkins. The napkins can be air dried and reused.

To begin, carefully remove three red bracts from the poinsettia bloom. Have a paper napkin ready to place the bracts on as they are removed, because they will begin dripping the milky sap immediately. Next, place one leaf inside a paper napkin, and cover the top of that leaf (or bract) with the other side of the napkin. (See figure.) Do this with the other two bracts. You are now ready to place the three napkins, containing one bract each, into the microwave oven, well separated from each other. Place an oven-proof custard cup over each napkin to weigh down the red bract and keep it from curling. Set the microwave oven for 1 minute at high heat. When the minute is up, remove custard cups, leaving napkins in place in the oven. The custard cups will be filled with moisture. Dry them out and replace them over the napkins containing the red bracts. Reset microwave oven for 1 minute more, at high heat, and continue drying the bracts for another minute. Then remove both custard cups and napkins to a flat surface. Carefully remove red poinsettia bracts from the wet napkins, and place each bract inside a dry paper napkin. Dry out interior of custard cups and return napkins and custard cups to the microwave oven for another minute of drying. Again, remove custard cups, dry out their interior, replace them over the napkins in the oven, and let bracts dry for two more minutes on high heat. When you remove the napkins from the oven, the bracts will be almost dry. Place them in dry paper napkins to continue drying overnight on a flat surface. By morning, they should be quite dry, quite flat, with a nice red coloring preserved.

Continue this method of drying until you have accumulated enough

This diagram shows three custard cups weighing down three paper napkins containing poinsettia bracts.

dry, red bracts, to be able to reconstruct your poinsettia bloom, in the mean-time keeping them free of exposure to moisture (away from vaporizers, tea kettles, and the like) until you have dried the stem to which you will be at-taching the red bracts. It is imperative that you not attach the bracts to the stem until you are certain it is quite thoroughly dry, as any moisture remain-ing in the stem will seep back into the bracts, causing them to lose color and shape. You will know when the stem is dry because, when you try to bend it, it will snap and will no longer emit any sap.

The stem from which you have been removing the bracts is now ready to dry. Cut it to a 4-inch length and place it on a piece of waxed paper to drain the milky sap from it. If you have a self-defrosting refrigerator, place the waxed paper containing the stem on top of it. The hot air from the defroster should dry the stem in about a week. Because the stem contains so much moisture, it will shrivel as it dries. This is not important, since only the beau-tiful flower will show once it is included in an arrangement.

To reconstruct the poinsettia bloom a thick white craft glue is quite good, as it allows you to place a bract at an angle and holds it in that position until dry. It is helpful, while replacing the bracts on the stem, to insert the stem in a bottle, glass, or block of floral foam to hold the entire flower up-right until all glue has dried.

The green leaves (or bracts) of the poinsettia should also be dried and used when reconstructing the bloom for a more natural appearance. Depend-ing on the size of the area where you will be displaying your preserved "rari-ty," you may only want to dry one to use as a focal point at the lower front of your arrangement. If you have a large foyer or other area calling for a large arrangement, you may want to dry five or seven blooms to use in a design that features poinsettias.

During the Christmas season, when poinsettia and mistletoe plants are at their peak of popularity, we often hear stories about the poisonous nature of these plants. In talking with Dr. George L. Wulster, Floraculture Specialist at Rutgers University, he assured me that both of these plants have been given a clean bill of health by the United States government. The Society of American Florists supplied me with test results of research carried out at the Ohio State University by Robert P. Stone and W. J. Collins, members of the Academic Faculty of Entomology there, concluding that the poinsettia is not harmful to humans or animal health if parts of the plant are ingested.

Similar research conducted by Richard Runyon, Department of Biolo-gy, Humboldt State University in Arcata, California, confirms that even oven-dried poinsettia plant material is without conclusive evidence of toxici-ty.

So, enjoy these beautiful natives of Mexico and spread the word that the poinsettia and mistletoe toxicity witch-hunt is over.

Pussy willow *(Salix discolor)*

When the wild pussy willow becomes alive with its tiny catkins in late Febru-ary, you can be certain that spring is on the way. You can usually find the wild variety where the ground is wet or damp. Be careful, because that is also the type of area in which poison sumac abounds.

My favorite willows are the sekko and corkscrew *(Salix matsudana),* Japanese varieties which grow in contorted shapes that intrigue me. If the branches are cut back severely every few years, they will produce even more luxuriant shapes, covered with even more catkins.

To dry these lovely, long-lasting branches, wait until the furry pussies have reached the size you desire. Cut the branches and arrange them in a tall, *dry* vase. If you add water to the vase, they will continue to develop and the gray, furry pips will turn into leaves.

Pussy willows look especially pretty when used in arrangements of daffodils and other spring flowers. The arrangement I made for this book of the madonna, on page 51, pictures this type of design.

Roses (*Rosa* species and hybrids)

Roses are a joy to preserve. They retain their "fresh picked" appearance and their sturdiness makes them easy to work with.

Before drying any rose, I sprinkle preheated silica gel inside its many petals, supporting the flower in my hand, and then empty the silica gel from the flower. This absorbs any dew or other moisture that may have been trapped in the depths of the bloom.

I then squeeze a few drops of Duco or other clear cement into the center of the rose. This adhesive is thin enough to run to the center of the petal structure to reinforce the flower at that vital point.

The rose should have a 2-inch stem on it and be dried, face up, so that silica gel crystals can be filtered in between each petal. Refer to the Quick Reference Chart for method and timing.

The roses I enjoy working with the most are: Tropicana, Queen, Elizabeth, Virgo, Garden Party, Tiffany, Chicago Peace, and Kings Ransome.

Dark red roses turn almost black, so, when I want a truly bright red rose, I dry a Tropicana which gives me that color. Garden Party dries more creamy than white and looks very much at home in colonial arrangements.

Santolina or lavender-cotton (*Santolina chamaecyparissus*)

Santolina is neither lavender nor cottony, but is an evergreen perennial from the Mediterranean, with silvery-gray aromatic leaves and yellow button-type single flowers. It is useful in dried arrangements and dries best by bunching and hanging to air dry.

Snowball (*Viburnum opulus* var. *sterilis*)

You may not have realized it, but this snowball tree is one of the many species of *Viburnum*. It has been called a shrub, bush, and tree by various horticulturists. Its blooms are look-alikes for the hydrangea, and the species, when in bloom, is oriental in appearance. It is a native of both China and Japan and blooms in this area in May and June.

When the flower heads sound papery to the touch, I cut them for air drying. Because their stems are so short, I insert an *S* hook between the florets, for hanging.

Starflower (*Scabiosa stellata*)

You are probably quite familiar with the tiny flowers that have exceptionally long, hairlike stems, known as "starflowers." They come in every color of the rainbow. They are commercially grown and dyed in Brazil and Italy. In 1980, a really different and unusual everlasting was introduced from Sweden, also under the name starflower. The new starflower does not resemble the familiar one at all. This one has a sphere-type head composed of little cell-like florets containing spiny, dark starlike centers. They are borne in profusion on sturdy 2-foot stems, are beige in color, about 1½ inches across the head, and provide an abundance of material for dried floral arranging.

(The Burpee Seed Company obtained this unique variety from the Botanical Garden in Uppsala, Sweden, and offered seeds to the American gardener for the first time last year.)

Starflowers are not grown for their rather insignificant looking fresh flowers, but for their dried flower heads, which can be picked in late summer or early fall when they are at their green-brown stage and before the seeds inside have shattered.

Their lovely shape and shade of beige make them especially welcome in a fall arrangement. I was intrigued by this newcomer to the dried flower scene, and experimented with bleaching them white and then dyeing them pastel shades for use at other times of the year. They withstood the bleaching operation quite well and I plan to use some of the white ball-type heads in winter and holiday arrangements. They also accepted a mild solution of alcohol dye and the colors dried clear and natural.

To bleach the starflower heads, I used pure household bleach, full strength, for twenty minutes. I then rinsed the flowers in a casserole of running water and inserted their stems in a block of floral foam to dry.

To grow starflowers, choose a sunny location with well-drained soil. Check seed packet for more information.

Starflowers can be bunched for air drying, or, by standing them upright in coffee cans, they will dry with less chance of damage to the heads. A wire stem inserted into their hollow stems will allow you to bend the stem once it is dry.

Sumac *(Rhus species)*

At just the mention of sumac, some people begin to itch. Evidently they are not aware that there are four varieties of sumac and only one is poisonous. The three good types look rather similar, producing thickly clustered, red, densely compacted berries, and they grow on dry land.

The poisonous variety *(Rhus vernix L.)* produces white berries that grow in loose and drooping clusters and only in swamps, bogs, and other wet places. All parts of this plant contain a dangerous skin irritant.

In the illustrations you can see how similar the smooth or highland sumac, staghorn, and dwarf varieties are. You can also see how it would be impossible to confuse them with the poison sumac.

For use in dried arrangements, the highland sumac *(Rhus glabra L.)* should be gathered in August or September, Quebec to British Columbia, Maine south to Florida, and even in California.

The staghorn sumac *(Rhus typhina L.)* is usually larger than the smooth sumac, and its flamelike, colored berries are ready for picking in August and September, from Nova Scotia to Quebec and Minnesota, south to northern Georgia and Tennessee and west to Iowa.

The dwarf sumac *(Rhus copallina L.)* produces its beautiful red berries for picking in September and October, just in time for our holiday decorating. It grows from southern Maine to New York, Michigan, central Wisconsin, and south to Florida and Texas. This variety is sometimes called "shining sumac" and is rich in tannin, used in tanning hides.

Few people realize that only the white-berried sumac is poisonous. These illustrations make it quite easy to see the difference in the four varieties. The first three types of sumac bear compacted red *berries. The poisonous plant bears loosely hanging* white *berries.*

All three types have branchlets of red berries which may be hung to dry. Run a piece of stem wire through the thick stem of the branchlet and out the other side, forming a hook with which to hang it.

When using sumac in an arrangement, I break the branchlets apart. Each heavy cluster of berries is made up of many smaller branches growing tightly together. The brighter berries are on the inside of the smaller branches, so I turn them around to show that side in my designs.

Tansy *(Tanacetum vulgare)*

Tansy grows wild throughout most of the United States and can be seen along the roadsides where the soil is heavy and neglected.

If you plant this perennial, do so along a fence row or at the back of your lot so it will not overrun your garden. It spreads quite a bit every year. It will grow from seed or root stock and blooms in late summer. Harvest the flower heads before they take on their rounded appearance, while they are still rather flat. These cheerful, yellow button flowers turn to a rich chocolate brown very soon after blooming, so pick some of the brown flowers too.

Tansy air dries well if you strip the leaves from the stems and hang it in small bunches, upside down in a well-ventilated area.

Tulips *(Tulipa* species and hybrids*)*

Although we generally think of tulips and Holland simultaneously tulips first delighted the gardeners of Turkey. For centuries, tulips were raised in great abundance in Turkey before the Austrian ambassador to that country took seeds to Vienna in 1554, introducing them to Europe at that time.

Tulips brighten our gardens mid-April through May. There are many varieties to choose from.

Most tulips retain their natural color when dried, except the reds, which dry darker. The red and yellow parrot tulip is one of my favorites for drying. The Darwins are the most difficult to dry because they are so large and thus tend to collapse easily.

Botanical tulips have many low-growing varieties, some reaching only 3 inches in height. They dry well and hold their shape well.

When planting, allow 6 inches between bulbs, and, on heavy land, cover them with 3 to 4 inches of soil. In lighter soil, cover the bulbs with 4 to 5 inches of earth. If the faded flowers are not removed before the seeds are set, the plant will not bloom the following year. Flower dryers seldom have this problem, because we are ready to pick the blooms as they open. Like the crocus and daffodils, the tulip leaves must be protected until they turn brown and die back, in order to feed the bulbs for next season's flowers.

To dry, the bloom should be cut as soon as it opens. Process the same as for daffodils, in preheated silica gel. If the stem stub still feels cool after the flower has dried, heat 1 inch of silica gel in a cup and set the stem end of the tulip in it for another day. To protect the flower from dampness during this process, keep the flower covered with a plastic bag. Refer to the Quick Reference Chart for additional information.

Since tulips close indoors, they are difficult to arrange attractively in fresh bouquets. However, if you will drop some melted candle wax—just a drop or two—in the center of each tulip, they will remain open. Since they only drink through the green part of their stem, cut off any white part of the stem end. This will keep the flowers fresh until you can work with them.

CARING FOR YOUR ARRANGEMENTS

Nostalgic, whimsical, and lovely to look at, dried flower arrangements are also quite delicate and brittle.

Heat, bright sun, and fluorescent lighting are enemies of all dried, natural materials, causing excessive brittleness and loss of color. Humidity is another foe of dried materials, because it can ruin perfectly preserved specimens, turning them limp, shapeless, and even moldy.

The following pointers will help you to enhance and extend the life of your preserved arrangements:

1. Store all dried materials at room temperature (not the attic or basement, which are generally prone to erratic temperature changes).

2. *Lightly* spray your arrangements, often, with a clear, acrylic, matte sealer. This treatment will increase the flowers' resistance to moisture (from the tea kettle or rainy day humidity seeping into the house), and will also freshen the appearance of the arrangement by concealing any dust that may have settled on the petals. Always spray outdoors on a clear, dry, still day. Hold the can of sealer at least 12 inches from the arrangement, so the spray will gently float in and around the various materials. If you spray too closely to the flowers, overspray can result, causing the flowers to look more plastic than natural. Several light sprayings are best, about five minutes apart.

3. If your design features woody cones and pods, or large sturdy flowers, such as zinnias, gently dust with an artist's watercolor brush.

4. If you have blended silk flowers into your dried floral design, they too will respond well to dusting with a small paintbrush.

5. Never use a vacuum cleaner on a dried or silk flower creation, lest it be whisked away to Never-Never Land! Although it takes a little patience to dust arrangements, and a little time to take them outdoors to the picnic table to spray them, it is well worth the effort, for you will be rewarded with many additional months or even years of enjoyment of the designs you have so lovingly created.

SOURCES FOR SUPPLIES

Supplies used in the projects in this book are obtainable at your local craft and hobby shops, home improvement centers, flower shops, or pharmacies. The additional sources for supplies listed here require a self-addressed, stamped envelope for a reply.

W. Atlee Burpee Co.
300 Park Ave.
Warminster, Pennsylvania 18991

Seeds, garden tools, excellent catalog.

Butterflies All, Inc.
P.O. Box 148
Chicago Park, California 95712

Butterflies and exotic moths.

Caswell-Massey Whiteheart Co.
9482 Dayton Way
Beverly Hills, California 90210

Potpourri ingredients, aromatics, fragrances.

Curtis Woodard
4150 Boulevard Pl.
Mercer Island, Washington 98040

Exotic pods, cones, dried materials.

Dried Flower Supplies
P.O. Box 601
Williamstown, New Jersey 08094

Wreath rings, floral foam, flowers, pods, cones, exotics from Africa and Australia, alum, ultra foam.

Floral Art Supplies, Inc.
P.O. Box 13273
Orlando, Florida 32859

Complete flower arranging supply house, silica gel, tools, books.

George W. Park Seed Co., Inc.
Greenwood, South Carolina 29646

Excellent catalog of seeds and plants.

Hazel Pearson Handicrafts
16017 E. Valley Blvd.
City of Industry, California 91744

Silica gel, floral supplies, complete craft supply house, ornaments, plaque boards, glue, catalog.

J. L. Hudson Co.
P.O. Box 1058
Redwood City, California 94064

Excellent seed catalog.

Lee Wards Creative Crafts, Inc.
1200 St. Charles St.
Elgin, Illinois 60120

Silica gel, floral supplies, baskets, dried flowers, birds, plaque boards, glue, craft supplies, catalog.

Morton Glass Works
Box 465
Morton, Illinois 61550

Stained glass kits.

Nature's Florist
R.D. 4 Nesco
Hammonton, New Jersey 08037

Dried wildlings, eastern seaboard cones and pods.

Takashimaya, Inc.
509 Fifth Ave.
New York, New York 10017

Pressed ferns.

W. J. Unwin, Ltd.
Box 9
Farmingdale, New Jersey 07727

Excellent seed catalog.

Van Bourgondien Bros.
P.O. Box A
Babylon, New York 11702

Bulbs and plants. Catalog.

Williamsburg Craft Center
Colonial Williamsburg Foundation
Williamsburg, Virginia 23185

Wall-pockets, colonial delft bricks, finger vases, brass containers, candlesticks, candles, books.

QUICK REFERENCE CHART

COMMON NAME	METHOD 1 AIR DRY	METHOD 2 SILICA GEL	METHOD 3 PREHEATED SILICA GEL	METHOD 4 MICROWAVE AND SILICA GEL	METHOD 5 MICROWAVE ONLY	METHOD 6 GLYCERIN SOLUTION	SPECIAL NOTES
Acacia	7 days	5 days	3 days	2 minutes	Flowers 2 minutes		Leaves and flowers also press well.
Achillea (Hybrid Yarrow)	5 days	3 days	1 ½ days	2 minutes			Golden dries best. Red loses color. Wild yarrow is lighter, so dries faster. I prefer air drying results.
African Daisy		5 days	3 days	2 minutes			Presses well also.
Ageratum	7 days	4 days	2 days	2 minutes			I prefer to air dry. Also presses well.
Ajuga	7 days	5 days	3 days	2 minutes		Leaves	Use either pink or blue varieties.
Althea (Rose of Sharon)		4 days	2 days	1 minute			Coat back of bloom with paraffin to reinforce. Woody pods are floral shape.
Alyssum, Sweet		4 days	2 days	2 minutes			Use either dwarf or tall varieties.
Ammobium	7 days						Pick before buds fully open.
Anemone		4 days	2 days	1 ½			Coat back with paraffin. Presses well.
Aster, China	7 days	5 days	3 days	2 minutes			Good results with air drying if flowers are fresh.

Plant							Comments
Aster, Laevis		4 days	2 days	1 ½ minutes			Pale blue remains unchanged.
Aster, Novi-Belgii		5 days	3 days	2 minutes			Pink becomes more lavender.
Azalea		3 days	1 ½ days	1 minute	Leaves	Leaves	Pink, white, and lavender colors remain true. Reinforce with wax and matte sealer.
Baby's Breath (all varieties including pink)	3 days					Flowers can be glycerinized by immersion.	Bristol fairy dries especially well as flowers are large. Pick when fully open for best results.
Bachelor's Button	5 days	3 days	1 ½ days	1 minute			I prefer air drying of freshly opened blooms.
Balsam		3 days	1 ½ days	1 minute			Pale pink holds true color.
Bells of Ireland	5 days	3 days	1 ½ days	1 minute			Dry when flowers are opened all the way to tip. I prefer air drying.
Bergamot		3 days	1 ½ days	1 minute			Pink remains true.
Black-eyed Susan	3 days	1 ½ days	1 minute	1 minute			Flower dries beautifully. Black centers are great in fall bouquets after plant goes to seed.
Bleeding Heart		3 days	1 ½ days	1 minute			Pink remains perfect.
Bluebell (all varieties)		3 days	1 ½ days	1 minute			Blue colors remain vibrant. Also press some.
Blue Salvia	5 days	3 days	2 days	1 minute	2 minutes 5 per napkin		Perfect blue. I prefer air drying.

COMMON NAME	METHOD 1 AIR DRY	METHOD 2 SILICA GEL	METHOD 3 PREHEATED SILICA GEL	METHOD 4 MICROWAVE AND SILICA GEL	METHOD 5 MICROWAVE ONLY	METHOD 6 GLYCERIN SOLUTION	SPECIAL NOTES
Boneset	5 days						White color dulls a bit.
Bouncing Bet		3 days	1 day	1 minute			White is clear.
Bridal Wreath	5 days	3 days	1 day	1 minute			I prefer air drying.
Butter-and-Eggs		3 days	1 day	1 minute			Yellow and orange is perfect. Resembles mini snapdragons.
Buttercup							Because bloom is so small, I prefer to press these.
Butterfly Weed	5 days	3 days	2 days	2 minutes			Bright orange dulls a bit. Sap runs from stem, so seal stem end with Saran before placing in silica gel. I prefer air drying.
Camellia		4 days	2 days	2 minutes	Leaves	Leaves	Pink remains true, red becomes darker.
Canada Thistle		3 days	2 days	2 minutes			Lilac dries true. Remove thorns from stems with sandpaper before drying.
Candytuft		3 days	1 ½ days	1 minute			Remains snowy white.
Carnation		4 days	2 ½ days	2 minutes			Pink and white dry best. Tie calyx with string before drying.
Catananche	5 days	3 days	1 ½ days	1 minute			Blues and yellows remain true.

Flower							Comments
Cattail	5 days						Pick for drying when you have to part leaves to find them.
Celosia	10 days				3 minutes		Place stems in bucket of water for 3 days before air drying. (See Facts about Flowers.)
Chamomile		3 days	1 ½ days	1 minute			Nice white.
Chrysanthemum (Most varieties)		7 days	4 days	2 minutes	Leaves	Leaves	Yellow-white and pink dry best. So many varieties — it is best to experiment.
Chrysanthemum (Button)		4 days	2 days	2 minutes	Leaves	Leaves	I like the white ones best.
Clematis		3 days	1 ½ days	1 minute	Leaves	Leaves	Blue ones keep color longest. Air dry pods and tendrils.
Columbine		3 days	1 ½ days	1 minute	Leaves	Leaves	Rose and blues dry well.
Coral Bells		3 days	1 ½ days	1 minute	Leaves	Leaves	Rosy delicate stems of bells.
Coreopsis		3 days	2 days	1 ½ minutes			Golden yellow remains true.
Cosmos		3 days	1 ½ days	1 minute			Dries and presses well.
Crape Myrtle	5 days	3 days	1 ½ days	1 minute	Leaves	Leaves	I prefer air drying. Color deepens but remains good.
Crocus		2 days	12 hours	1 minute			See Facts about Flowers for more information.
Curled Dock	5 days						Refer to Air Drying section.

COMMON NAME	METHOD 1 AIR DRY	METHOD 2 SILICA GEL	METHOD 3 PREHEATED SILICA GEL	METHOD 4 MICROWAVE AND SILICA GEL	METHOD 5 MICROWAVE ONLY	METHOD 6 GLYCERIN SOLUTION	SPECIAL NOTES
Daffodil		2 days	12 hours	1 minute			Read Facts about Flowers for more information.
Dahlia (Dwarf)		4 days	2 days	2 minutes		Leaves	Red Wiek variety darkens but is worth drying.
Daisy, African		3 days	1 ½ days	1 minute			Clear yellow is retained.
Daisy, English		3 days	1 day	1 minute	Leaves		Pink and white dry best.
Daisy, Gloriosa		4 days	2 days	2 minutes			Strong yellow.
Daisy, Marguerite		5 days	3 days	2 minutes			Beautiful white. Reinforce back with wax.
Daisy, Oxeye		3 days	1 ½ days	1 minute			These press well if placed between wax paper and stepped on to flatten center first.
Daisy, Painted		6 days	4 days	2 minutes			Yellow, white, blue, and pink remain clear.
Daisy, Shasta		3 days	1 ½ days	1 minute			Good white.
Day Lily		5 days	3 days	2 minutes			Needs reinforcement with glue around stem area and painting with wax on entire back of flower.
Delphinium	5 days	3 days	1 ½ days	1 minute		Leaves	I prefer to air dry tall spires and silica gel dry florets.

Flower						Comments
Dogwood		3 days	1 days	1 minute	Leaves	Pink turn purplish.
Echinops	5 days	3 days	1 ½ days			I prefer air drying.
English Bluebell		4 days	2 days	2 minutes		Lovely pale blue.
Euonymus		3 days	1 ½ days	1 minute	Leaves	Pale green.
Feverfew		3 days	2 days	1 minute		Good white.
Forget-me-not		3 days	1 ½ days	1 minute		Bright blue. Presses well also.
Freesia		3 days	1 ½ days	1 minute		White and yellow true. Orange becomes darker.
Gaillardia		3 days	2 days	2 minutes	Leaves	Red and yellow flowers darken a little.
Geranium	5 days					Individual florets press beautifully.
Globe Amaranth	5 days				2 minutes	Refer to Facts about Flowers.
Goldenrod	5 days					Refer to Facts about Flowers.
Grape Hyacinth		4 days	2 days	2 minutes		Retains medium blue to dark blue color. Presses well, too.
Heather	5 days	3 days	1 ½ days			Pink runs to dusty rose and lavender retains color.
Helichrysum (Strawflower)	5 days					All colors dry well, in upright position.

COMMON NAME	METHOD 1 AIR DRY	METHOD 2 SILICA GEL	METHOD 3 PREHEATED SILICA GEL	METHOD 4 MICROWAVE AND SILICA GEL	METHOD 5 MICROWAVE ONLY	METHOD 6 GLYCERIN SOLUTION	SPECIAL NOTES
Helipterum	5 days						Strong yellow. Papery.
Hens & Chicks		11 days	9 days	3 minutes			Interesting rosettes for use on plaques, etc.
Hyacinth		5 days	2 days	1 minute			Individual florets only.
Hydrangea	5 days Full head	3 days Florets	2 days Florets	1 minute Florets			Refer to Facts about Flowers.
Joe-Pye-Weed	5 days						If picked early retains bright lavender rose color.
Jonquil		2 days	12 hours	1 minute			Refer to Daffodil in Facts about Flowers.
Johnny-Jump-Up							I prefer to press these due to their size.
Larkspur	5 days	3 days	1½ days	1 minute			White, blue, pink retain excellent color. I prefer air drying.
Lavender	5 days	3 days	1½ days	1 minute			Lavender color remains excellent.
Liatris	5 days	4 days	2 days	2 minutes			Rosy lavender color unchanged. Because of their size I air dry most.
Lilac	6 days	5 days	3 days	2 minutes			Lavender, white of common, and deep purple of French dry with excellent shape and color. Refer to Facts about Flowers.

Name							Notes
Lily of the Valley		4 days	2 days	1 minute Flowers	Leaves	Leaves	Both pink and white dry to perfection. Check Foliage section for drying leaves.
Lobelia							Best pressed.
Love-in-a-Mist		3 days	1 day	1 minute			Delicate blue and pink flowers dry perfectly. Let some go to seed for exotic pods.
Lunaria	5 days					1 week	Air drying or glycerinizing is best. Refer to Air Drying section for more information.
Lupines Mahonia		4 days	2 days	1 ½ minute		Leaves	Glossy leaves glycerinize well.
Mallow		3 days	1 ½ days	1 minute			Lovely pink flowers, need reinforcing with wax.
Marsh Mallow		3 days	1 ½ days	1 minute			White and rose dry well. Require reinforcing. Pods are brown wooden flowers.
Marigold, Single Dwarf		4 days	2 days	2 minutes			Yellow and brown flowers darken a little.
Marigold, Nugget	10 days	7 days	4 days	3 minutes			Gold and orange flowers dry perfectly. Reddish become a bit dark.
Marigold, Climax	12 days	8 days	5 days	4 minutes	Leaves		Beautiful shape and color are retained. Used in arrangement in this book. The "air dried" flatten some but color is perfect.
Marigold, Senator Dirksen	12 days	8 days	5 days	4 minutes	Leaves		Retain shape and color. Air dried loses shape but retains color and is good at side and back of arrangement.

COMMON NAME	METHOD 1 AIR DRY	METHOD 2 SILICA GEL	METHOD 3 PREHEATED SILICA GEL	METHOD 4 MICROWAVE AND SILICA GEL	METHOD 5 MICROWAVE ONLY	METHOD 6 GLYCERIN SOLUTION	SPECIAL NOTES
Mimosa		3 days	1 ½ days	1 minute	Leaves		Filamentous stamens retain puff-ball appearance if dry when put in silica gel. They press well, too.
Mock Orange		3 days	1 ½ days	1 minute	Leaves		Creamy white blossoms dry so perfectly that even the tiny centers are fresh looking.
Mountain Laurel						Leaves	Flowers have a sticky coating to which the silica gel adheres. Leaves are beautiful in arrangement.
Nigella		3 days	1 day	1 minute			Delicate blue and pink flowers dry perfectly. Let some go to seed for exotic pods.
Passionflower		3 days	2 days	1 minute			Dries perfectly. Wax back of petals.
Pansy		5 days	2 days	1 minute		Leaves	Colors dry true, even dark purple varieties dry well. Leave 2-inch stem attached. Also press some.
Pearly Everlasting	5 days				1 to 2 minutes		I also dry these in the microwave *without* silica gel.
Peony		5 days	3 days	2 minutes	Leaves	Leaves	White, pink, and red retain perfect color. See Facts about Flowers.
Pinks, Dianthus		3 days	1 ½ days	2 minutes			Perfect color. See Carnations in Facts about Flowers.

Pyracantha	5 days				Creamy flowers make an unusual filler.
Queen Anne's Lace	5 days	3 days	2 days	1 minute	Lacy, delicate bloom dries perfectly. I prefer Method 3.
Roses		5 days	3 days	2 minutes	See Facts about Flowers.
Santolina, Lavender-Cotton	5 days	3 days	1 ½ days	1 minute	Pretty yellow. Use several together for best effect.
Sea Lavender	5 days				Lavender-tinged, delicate filler.
Sedum, Donkey Tail	12 days	10 days	5 days	2 minutes	Yellow flowers with strong stems.
Snapdragon		7 days	4 days	2 minutes	Yellow, white, pink dry true.
Spanish Bayonet Yucca		3 days	1 ½ days	1 minute	Creamy bells dry well individually. Leaves air dry.
Spirea	5 days				Air dries best.
Statice, *Limonium sinuatum*	5 days			Refer to Method 6	Yellow, rose, blue, apricot, purple, and white.
Statice, German *Tatarica*	5 days				Comes in white only and is a prized filler. Can be grown here as a biennial.
Stephanotis		3 days	1 ½ days	1 minute	White turns a lovely ivory.
Stokesia		4 days	2 days	1 minute	Lavender-blue is true when dried.

COMMON NAME	METHOD 1 AIR DRY	METHOD 2 SILICA GEL	METHOD 3 PREHEATED SILICA GEL	METHOD 4 MICROWAVE AND SILICA GEL	METHOD 5 MICROWAVE ONLY	METHOD 6 GLYCERIN SOLUTION	SPECIAL NOTES
Sunflower		4 days	2 days	2 minutes			These old-fashioned flowers dry perfectly.
Sweet William		3 days	2 days	1 ½ minutes			Pink, white, and red dry well and press well too.
Tansy	5 days				3 minutes		Sturdy, woody button type. See Facts about Flowers.
Tithonia		3 days	2 days	1 ½ minutes			Dries a perfect bright orange.
Tulips		3 days	2 days	1 minute			See Facts about Flowers.
Viburnum	5 days Berries				Leaves	Leaves	Leatherleaf viburnum leaves are especially beautiful.
White Snakeroot	5 days						Resembles blue ageratum. Air dries to a good white.
Wind Flowers		(See Anemone)					
Winged Everlasting	5 days						Resembles mini-daisies with yellow centers.
Xeranthemum	3 days						Pale pink, white, and lavender. Papery-type.
Yarrow	5 days						Wild white, gold hybrid, or brown wild.
Zinnia	4 days	4 days	2 days	2 minutes			Sturdy. Reds darken but most colors dry true. See Facts about Flowers.

METRIC CONVERSION CHART

	True Metric	Approximate Metric
¼ inch	6.35 mm	6 mm
⅜ inch	9.5 mm	1 cm
1 inch	2.54 cm	2.5 cm
2 inch	5.08 cm	5 cm
3 inch	7.62 cm	7.5 cm
4 inch	10.16 cm	10 cm
5 inch	12.70 cm	12.5 cm
6 inch	15.24 cm	15.25 cm
7 inch	17.78 cm	17.75 cm
8 inch	20.32 cm	20.5 cm
9 inch	22.86 cm	22.75 cm
10 inch	25.4 cm	25.5 cm
12 inch	30.48 cm	30.5 cm

INDEX